TIME
&
DISTANCE

BOOK THREE

THE LOVE STORY OF

NANCY & FRANK

November 2019
Nancy Lou Henderson

NANCY LOU HENDERSON

NLH PRESS

TIME & DISTANCE
Book Three
The Love Story of Nancy & Frank

© 2019 by Nancy Lou Henderson

www.NancyLouHenderson.com

facebook.com/nancy.henderson.39

twitter.com/nlhende49

NLH Books

All rights reserved.

This book or parts thereof may not be reproduced in any form, stored in a retrieval system, or transmitted in any form by any means—electronic, mechanical, photocopy, recording, or otherwise—without prior written permission of the publisher, except as provided by the United States of America copyright law.

ISBN 978-16999171-8-3

Printed in the United States of America.

Dedication

to frank

Table of Contents

1 two weeks of heaven 1
2 back to missing him 9
3 where are his letters? 19
4 padlock and key 31
5 disposition form letter 40
6 man's love not a weakness 51
7 guard duty & thoughts on war 61
8 poem to my wife 71
9 love explained 80
10 dearest fancy 89
11 wife of a shorty 99
12 last days are scary 107
13 getting closer to you 115
14 a message in a letter 122
15 leaving the army behind us 131
16 deciding our future 137
Stay Tuned! 145
Also by Nancy Lou Henderson 146
Preview: Faith & Eternity 147
About the Author 155

TIME & DISTANCE

BOOK THREE

THE LOVE STORY OF

NANCY & FRANK

And fare thee weel, my only luve!
And fare thee weel awhile!
And I will come again, my luve,
Though it were ten thousand mile.

— *"A Red, Red Rose," Robert Burns*

1

two weeks of heaven

THE LOVE STORY OF NANCY & FRANK

Standing in our living room, holding the phone to my ear, then hearing Frank's voice saying he loved me, was surreal. For the first time in six months, I was actually talking to Frank and it felt like it was all a dream. How had he called me? Where was he?

It took only seconds before Frank answered all of my questions with his next words, "Nancy, I am in California and I am fixing to get on a flight to Houston. Wanna come and pick me up at the Houston airport?"

I was fighting back tears, holding back squealing loudly, and smiling from ear to ear all at one time but I managed to tell him, "You betcha, I do! I love you so much."

Frank told me his flight number and what time he would be landing in Houston then we laughed and talked together like a couple of giddy kids until Frank's flight number was called. Neither of us wanted to be the first to hang up the phone, so we told each other how much we loved each other, and we decided to count to three together then hang up at the same time.

After we hung up, I was so excited that I decided to call my folks, wake them up, then tell them that Frank was coming home, and I would shortly be heading to the airport in Houston.

Since it was an hour and a half trip to the airport, I quickly jumped into the shower then got dressed. Gosh, it felt like I was in a dream. I kept pinching myself but definitely not wanting to wake up if it was just a dream. I was trying to fix my hair, but I kept jumping up and down from my excitement and looking up at the ceiling saying, "Thank you, God! Thank you, God!"

Finally, I was ready to leave the house and drive to the airport in Houston. I was so excited that while driving I was laughing, squealing, and fidgeting in the seat a little, might want to make that a lot!

I arrived at the airport close to the time that Frank's plane would be landing. After parking the car, I literally ran to the entrance of the terminal. As much as I had come to hate being at the airport, this time I was actually picking up my heart and soul, my "Dimples."

Just as Frank's plane landed, I made it to the gate where Frank would unload the plane. My heart was beating so fast. In only minutes I would see him walk down that ramp tunnel into the room. I kept looking into the tunnel to catch a glimpse of him then there he was smiling ear to ear!

When Frank exited the tunnel I ran towards him, he dropped his bag, I jumped into his arms, and as we kissed he held me tightly as we rotated round and round. Just being able to physically touch each other was indescribable. Frank placed me gently back on the ground but never let go of my hand as he picked up his bag.

Frank had only brought the one carry-on bag home with him, so we did not have to go to baggage claim. We ran holding hands to the car and left the airport. Frank drove, and I was his "shotgun" in the Super Beetle. Frank had his arm around me as I tried to sit as close to him as those bucket seats would allow. I was practically sitting in his lap. It seemed we just couldn't get close enough to each other.

Frank told me that he tried to be strong and think about our future after getting out of the Army and not spending the money to take an R&R, but he just couldn't do it. He decided saving money was not worth it because he needed to see me, and I needed to see him. Of course, I totally agreed with him.

We decided to stop at a restaurant to eat breakfast and we each ordered the biggest breakfast they could fit on a platter. We had fried eggs, bacon, sausage, biscuits, grits, gravy, jelly, hash browns, and orange juice, with lots of coffee on the side. Frank told me that he thought he was in Heaven eating all of that good food.

Frank looked so tired, but he was smiling from ear to ear. It had been a very long flight from Vietnam to Texas with lots of stops along the way. He was also very tan which was so different for my redhead with freckles.

Frank noticed fairly quickly how thin I had gotten and told me he would have to see about fattening me up while he was home and I think it was already working because I ate every piece of food on the plates the waitress brought out to our table.

It seemed like every worry in the world has just been taken from me and from Frank's smile I knew he felt the same way. We finished eating breakfast then headed to Van Vleck to our little white frame house. It was still dark outside as we pulled up to our home.

Once we got inside the house, Frank asked me if we had hot water because he wanted to take a hot shower and get Vietnam off his skin. I told him that we definitely did have hot water. Frank took off his uniform then went into the bathroom. I hung up his uniform and got some of his civvies for him to wear.

Frank yelled from the bathroom, "Lou, do we have any guy soap?"

I went into the bathroom and opened the cabinet to get out his favorite soap then went to the shower curtain to give Frank the soap. Frank grabbed my hand and pulled me into the shower—fully clothed! I could not help but laugh standing in that shower getting soaking wet in my clothes. Of course, Frank was laughing from the moment he grabbed my hand and pulled me into that shower.

His next words were, "I can't reach my back, so I thought like a good wife you would want to wash it for me".

I told him, "Of course, that's what you were thinking, Dimples."

About eight o'clock that morning, we decided to drive to Bay City to let my work know that I would not be there for a couple of weeks. I really did not care how they reacted because no matter what, I would not work one day while Frank was home. It ended up that they were very excited to meet him, and they had no problem with me being off.

After that Frank and I returned to our home to take a nap. It had been a long night with so many beautiful emotions and we were exhausted. There are no words for the feeling of having Frank hold me while we fell asleep. It had been six long months since we had held and laid so close to each other but suddenly it felt like it had only been yesterday. A feeling that is unforgettable forever.

Of course, we saw Frank's folks and mine that day, but I don't remember the exact sequence of the afternoon. It seems the main thing I remember was being with Frank and holding his hand in mine tightly.

The next day, Frank and I traveled to Hico, Texas, where they were holding the Blakley Family Reunion which was always held near the 4th of July. We visited with so many kinfolks there then we returned to Van Vleck the next day.

Frank and I made that trip he had mentioned in his letter to the beach one night and walked hand in hand next to the water. It was a beautiful night and the water was like glass softly rippling to the sand on the shore. We put a blanket on the sand then talked for hours sitting there in the moonlight. We had so much to talk about. We had missed just being able to talk and dream together.

Time was passing too fast, but we were trying to not think about the day that Frank would have to leave to go back to Vietnam. We wanted to make every second we had together count but it was always in the back of our minds that he would have to leave to go back.

We spent a lot of time listening to music on our reel-to-reel. Sometimes we would place a blanket on the floor and eat fruit, cheese, summer sausage, and crackers while we listened to music. Sometimes we would slow dance together around the living room holding each other tightly. We had a need to hold each other as much as possible and for as long as possible, so the feeling would stay with us for the months of separation ahead.

The day before Frank was to leave to go back to Vietnam, he and I went to see a movie called "Love Story." He had asked me in a letter to read the book, but I had not done it yet, so we went to see the movie. That was a terrible mistake because I cried for an hour. Frank did not know that it would affect me so strongly, was devastated, and apologized for taking me to see it but I told him that in the movie it was said, "Love means never having to say you're sorry." Seeing how upset that Frank was at my crying, I dried my tears and realized that I had to show him how strong I could be.

Early on the morning of July 15, 1971, Frank and I returned with others to the airport in Houston. This is the only time that I do not remember saying goodbye to Frank. I do not know why but I think it was, I chose to forget it. I do remember thinking when Frank was home that God had let him live to come home to see me again, but I was afraid it was because Frank would not live to come home again.

Once Frank got back to Vietnam we would start over the whole process of waiting for letters from each other.

The first letter I received from Frank was written on July 15, 1971. The airline had put him up for the night in the Carlton Hotel in Hong Kong.

July 15, 1971
Dearest Nancy,
Hi Honey. Well, I made it this far. I got into Hong Kong about 9:00 pm tonight and Pan Am, sent me over to this hotel. I'll stay the night and get up at 6:00 am and leave the hotel at 7:15 am. Breakfast is included as well as transportation.

Pretty nice of them I thought. I figured I had to sleep in the airport because I sure wasn't going to pay for a place to stay. Everything has gone fine so far.

I'm about worn out from so much flying and sitting and a cold I got from somewhere that has gone to my ears and making me very miserable, isn't helping either. HA!

Nancy, I want to tell you one more time how much I loved the few days that we had together. I love you so much Darling and every moment with you was a blessing. I miss your warmth and love so much already.

Nancy, there are so many things that I wanted to say to you and do for you that didn't get said or done. I guess these things you feel without me having to say them or do them. I feel we have such an understanding and devoted love. That's the way it should be.

I love you, Nancy and I hope you realize that and treasure my love as I treasure yours. I have to close now because it's late and also, I'm getting kind of very sad. I miss you, my Darling and love you so very much. Take care of yourself because you belong to me. OK? OK!

All my love for you, my Wife,
Frank

THE LOVE STORY OF NANCY & FRANK

I know I cried when I got the above letter. We were not meant to be separated but we knew we had survived the first six months and we would be even stronger for the next six months. We were two hearts beating as one with a love for each other that could not be broken but would grow stronger and stronger because it was eternal.

2

back to missing him

Our two weeks together had come to an end and Frank had returned to Vietnam. There is really no way to explain the feeling of having had Frank home for two weeks, having to tell him goodbye again, then knowing it would be six months before seeing him, talking to him, and holding him in my arms again. The best words I have to explain this feeling would be, "Feeling like your heart had been torn in half."

Our love for each other had grown stronger with every day we were apart the first six months and we knew that we were connected in more than letters. Our hearts and souls had connected in a magical way which let us feel each other's thoughts as they actually happen.

While Frank was home, I told him all about what the doctor had said and the tests that I had done at the hospital in Wharton. I had a test to check to see if I had a blockage in my fallopian tubes that would prevent ovulation from happening. Frank's Mom had gone with me for this test. This test was done without anesthesia. A tube was inserted into my uterus and a dye was pumped into the fallopian tubes while X-rays were taken to see if the dye went through the tubes and passed into the uterine cavity.

This test is called a Hysterosalpingogram or (HSG). It was a very painful test causing cramping during and after with a feeling of nausea and dizziness. The doctor talked to me constantly during the test telling me when to breathe and trying to help me relax. He told me that childbirth would not be any worse than this test and years later that would prove to be true.

The test showed that there was not any blockage in my fallopian tubes which gave Frank and I a lot of hope in trying to have a child. The doctor also told me that the test might just help with fertility. Of course, I did not know that Frank would be coming home on an R&R. When he surprised me by coming home, we decided while he was home on R&R, it just might be our time to conceive a child.

The next letter I received from Frank was started one day then finished on the next. We were in the process of waiting for letters to arrive again. Of course, Frank had letters waiting for him when he arrived back to Phu Bai, but they were written by me before he surprised me by coming home on R&R.

August 5 - 6 1971
Dear Nancy,
Good Morning Honey. Yeah, I'm writing this letter at 11:00 am in the morning. I'm off today. This time I had only twenty-one days accrued toward a break. I tried making you a tape, but I couldn't get the microphone to work.

Honey, I don't know if we'll be able to meet in California or not. We've heard some word that they are closing Oakland down and that now everyone is going through Ft. Lewis, Washington. I don't know if this is true or not, but we should find out in the next couple of months. If we can't meet in California, I want you to tell me where you would like to go instead. Or if you want, we could just meet in Houston and live in a hotel for a while and see Houston. It's up to you.

Hey, I love you, Nancy. You still love me, don't you? I hope you do because I love you so very much Nancy. My whole world is built around you and only you. Honey, I'm going to close now and go check my mail and see if I got a letter from you, so I can answer some of your more recent questions. See you in about thirty minutes. Don't go away.

I'm back a day later but I'm back. I'm sorry it's taking me so long to finish this letter, but I was so down after getting no mail yesterday for the fourth day in a row that I just couldn't write. I'm sorry but I hope you'll understand.

Hey, you, you still love me? You'd better cause I'm not letting you go, no matter what. So, what do you think about that? I hope it's alright because if it's not then tough luck. I'm afraid you're stuck with me no matter what, so you might as well get to like it.

Honey, I have to close for now because it's 1:00 am in the morning and I have to get up soon, so please, please take care of yourself and keep loving me as you do now. God bless you, my love, and take care of you for me.

Your Faithful, Loving, and Devoted Husband,
Frank

I really hated reading a letter from Frank saying he was not receiving my letters because it always ended up with him doubting in his mind my love for him. I loved him with all of my heart and he knew that but when the mail was slow he would fall into the trap of doubt.

After being two weeks late for mother nature to come for a visit, I wrote Frank a letter telling him that we just might have succeeded in conceiving a child.

August 8, 1971
Dear Lou,
Hello, my Darling. I hope this day finds you well and in good health, only maybe a little fatter. Your health and wellbeing are most important to me. If I know your well and feeling fine then that's less to worry me. So, promise you'll take care of yourself and get enough rest and eat right too. That's an order from the chief. You're all I got

Honey and I won't permit you to be sick. But I do need a little help from you, so I'm asking you, please.

I got the cigarette maker today and thanks very much. Just in time too, the PX only has Salem and you know how I feel about cigarettes. Darling, you make me so very happy and proud of you. You do everything you can to take care of me. Thank you for being my wife. I love you, Nancy.

Honey, I have to confide in you about this baby thing. All along I've not wanted to give you a hint that I'm really excited because if it doesn't turn out I don't want you hurt or disappointed. I know how much a child means to you and believe me it means very much to me too.

Anyway, I've tried to hide my excitement and anxiety for your sake. It's almost like lying to you. I can't do it anymore. I'm making myself miserable as Hades. So now I'm going to level with you. I still don't want you to feel that you've let me down or I'm upset about it if it doesn't work out the way we feel. I won't be. I'll be a bit disappointed but that's to be expected. So please don't be so down if it doesn't work out. OK?

Well okay, here goes. First off, I too feel you're pregnant. Maybe it's because I want to feel this way because I want you to be. Anyway, I really do feel you are. I don't know why. It's something I couldn't put my finger on, but I still feel it. I'm almost afraid to believe it because I'm afraid if I do and I really want something, I won't get it.

I want to be able to say to myself that yes, yes, yes, it's true. It's happening. You promise to tell me as soon as you know either way? Please. Once again I want you to promise me you'll take it like I know you should, and I promise you, I'll take it like, I should.

Nancy, since I've been home and come back through your letters, you seem more grown up and mature than you ever were. I too seem more mature, to myself that is. Maybe we're growing up together and maturing with one another. The funny thing is that when something matures it's supposed to get old and worn. Our love has done nothing but grown and get stronger.

I wonder if our love for one another will ever reach a limit where it stops getting better and stronger? I really can't see that day ever coming. How can something that is so alive and beautiful ever get stale and dormant? Not possible, huh? I don't think so either, so I just hope my poor old full heart can take it without bursting apart.

Well, I have to close cause it's going on 10:00 pm and I got a big bad 12 hours tonight. God bless you my Darling because I love you so very much. Good night my love and dream of our life to come.

All my Love for you, my Wife,
Frank
P.S. Keep making those booties. We'll use them someday.

I am so glad that I have this letter to share with you all. Frank loved children and I knew this. I also knew that he wanted a child as much as I did. What Frank did not like was that I would cry heartbroken and blame myself when it ended up I was not pregnant. Frank loved me so much and did not ever want to see me cry or be heartbroken. So, to keep from showing me his disappointment, he would put his feelings aside and try really hard to act like it did not matter to him, but I knew.

We knew everything about each other. Couples who love each other and are connected so deeply by heart and soul cannot help but know how each other feel about everything. We wanted to share our love with a child and teach that child what love was really about.

At the risk of getting in serious trouble, Frank wrote his next letter to me while he was at work.

> *August 13, 1971*
> *Dear Lou,*
> *Good morning my love. How's my wife today? I hope she's loving me as much as I'm loving her.*
> *Honey, I'm sorry, I haven't written for a couple of days, but they've been working our _ _ _ es off. I'm writing this at work at 5:00 am in the morning, so it has to be short.*
> *I feel bad about not being able to write but I hope you know that I'll write when I can. We're really short of people and as I said, they're working us almost around the clock.*
> *They gave out ETS (Expiration Term of Service) drops of thirty days. So, I went running down to see if I got one. I was really excited when I heard they were but as usual, I struck out. They were for September, October, and November. I haven't given up yet. I plan on being home by Christmas, one way or the other. Now if I can only convince the Army of that.*
> *Well, I'd better close before I get caught not working again. Please take care of yourself and keep loving me as you always have. God bless you and keep you safe for me.*
> *All My Love,*
> *Frank*

God has a season and a time to every purpose under Heaven. It was not our season or time to have a child. Mother nature decided to pay me a visit three weeks late and I tearfully wrote Frank a letter to let him know that I was not pregnant. It was a very hard letter to write because I knew in my heart how disappointed he would be.

I had not received Frank's letter from August the 8th yet but the very day he wrote the letter telling me how he really felt about having a child, mother nature came to pay me a visit and I wrote a letter telling him we were not having a baby.

Frank received the letter I wrote to him about not being pregnant on the same day I received his letter telling me how much he wanted a child. In two different places, miles apart from each other, we were both getting letters revealing deep feelings. It was not a good day for either one of us, but God was with us.

In my letter, I told Frank that I thought that the if we wanted to be parents, we needed to check into adoption. We had been married over three years and I thought that God wanted us to be loving parents of an adopted child who would be ours and needed to know the kind of love God had put in our hearts.

The adoption process would take a long time and it could take us years to adopt a child, so the process would need to be started as soon as we could. It was also very expensive with lots of paperwork.

The writing in Frank's next letter is not good. He is visibly upset in his writing and just by looking at the letter you can see the deep emotions and feel them.

> *August 14, 1971*
> *Dear Nancy,*
> *Dear Nancy, again. Why? Because you're so dear to me. That's why. You know, I received three letters from you today and I read them in order and the last one was*

when you found out that you weren't pregnant. You said you started your period.

You wanted to ask me a question that you said was very important. You were right. It is very important, and I really appreciated you asking me. It's important to me too. I want you to go to the Methodist Home in Waco when you can and see what the requirements for adopting a baby will be. I want to know because if I can't give you a child naturally, I'll do everything in my power to give you an adopted child. I'll be more than happy to.

Honey, I know how much a family means to you and I'm sure you understand just how much it means to me, so let's have our first child now. You know I'll love an adopted child as much as our own. So, please find out and I'll send my whole paycheck home or anything, I promise. You want to start our family now and you want to adopt a child so that's fine with me. Let's do it, Honey.

Darling, I'm sorry this happened the way it did. I was afraid that we'd both be disappointed if it didn't happen but we both should have known but dreams happen. So, what, huh? Good. At least we know now for sure. Right? I'm just sorry you're having the cramps so bad and are really having a bad time. I only wish I was there to comfort you and tell you everything was alright.

I'm sorry I'm so far away and can't be there. I know that this letter may not be much comfort to you because it'll be five days late when you get it and my words will be stale, but I want you to know that I do care and am concerned about you. Darling, you are all I have, and I want you to be ok.

So, check and see what the requirements are, and we'll adopt a child, I promise. You asked me not to fuss at you, just understand you. Honey, you know I'll understand when you're really down and upset. I understand, I really do. How can I fuss at you over something that I'm so strong about? Honey, I love you so much and understand you and I know exactly how you feel, so you know I'll always understand you.

Don't worry about me fussing at you because I know when you need sympathy and when you need fussing and I know you need my understanding now and I hope that I have provided it. Honey just remember that no matter what happens, that I love you and I'll always love you forever and ever. If you'll just remember that and find strength in it then we'll forever find peace and love and happiness.

God bless you and may he please protect you and keep you well till I'm physically able to do it for myself. I love you, my Darling.

All my love, devotion, and understanding,
Frank
P.S. Please let me know about the adoption process as soon as possible.

Frank was right when he wrote, "At least we know." This time it would not be a three-month to a four-month ordeal of waiting to find out. God spared us that and we were grateful. Frank and I were very strong individuals but together we had a strength that was unbeatable and unbreakable.

I wrote the Methodist Home in Waco for information on adoption and I sent Frank the information. We knew this would not happen overnight but could possibly take years.

To everything, there is a season, and time to every purpose under Heaven...

3

where are his letters?

It was hard to keep my mind on my work after Frank left to go back to Vietnam, but I knew each day that passed was one less day he had left in Vietnam and the Army. We had now gone past the halfway mark in Frank's days left in Vietnam which was the main thing on our minds.

Frank was right when he said that it would be hard for him to come home then leave again to go back to Vietnam. Our communication through letters was all that we had and when that communication was disrupted, we would both get very upset.

I have responded to the following letters with what I recall that I wrote to Frank. I did not receive these letters with his replies for over two weeks after they were written by him. Frank was receiving my letters then writing to me, but I was not getting mail from him. I am mentioning this before the letters to help you understand the last letters in this chapter.

In the next letter, Frank was really down but both of us were trying to deal with separation and disappointment at the same time.

> *August 17, 1971*
> *Dear Nancy,*
> *How are you today? I hope you are in better spirits and are feeling better than you have been. You know how I've felt about the trials and troubles you've been going through. I just wish that I could have been there to comfort you and help you through it. You know how I feel and so let's just forget it and start planning for us when I get out.*
>
> *Believe it or not, we're getting out in 151 days. Only 151 days. It's a long way from 1460 days that we started with. I'm starting to feel a little short.*

WHERE ARE HIS LETTERS?

I'm getting depressed trying to think of things to says, so I'm going to have to close and try again later. I just know one thing and that's, that I love you and I want to be by your side for always and never leave you for anything.

Please take care of yourself and write me when you can. Please try to be happy and be patient. I love you, Nancy.

All My Love,
Frank
P.S. I love you.

I knew that Frank was having a terrible time since returning to Vietnam. Coming home then returning to a place that was so awful had to have been terrible. Knowing Frank as a very strong person, I knew that he would gather the strength inside him and work through his feelings to come out of his depression.

As Frank's wife, I knew that it was my responsibility to pull myself together and help get his spirits up quickly. I decided to write him a letter that would definitely perk him up, get his mind off of Nam, lessen his worry about me, make him smile big dimples, and quite possibly make him laugh out loud in disbelief.

I had never written Frank a "suggestive" letter ever, but I decided to give it my best shot, partly to just catch him off guard and by surprising the heck out of him. Seems, I succeeded.

August 18, 1971
Dear Nancy,
Howdy wife! You had to go, and do it didn't you? You just had to mention it! Couldn't just kind of ignore

it and let me not think about it, now could you. No! You had to mention It!

Good grief Honey. I don't know if I'll be able to stand it and wait to get home for another four months and 27 hours. HA! HA! Just believe me, when I get home I'm going to hold you to your words.

Seriously, Honey, I'm so glad to see your spirits a bit improved. You never quit surprising me. Once again you've proven that you're a strong woman and you're able to face reality. You're made of love and understanding. What more could I as for in a woman that I want to spend the rest of my life with?

I love you so much Darling and I'll never ever regret our marriage. I love you more and more each day that passes. I'm stammering and stuttering trying to find the right words so that you could get some idea of just how much I love you. I seem to say the same words over and over in each letter but I'm not good at expressing myself.

Just believe in me and my love because we both know what we share is real and will never falter or fail. I must close now because I'm writing this at lunchtime and I have to go back to work now. I love you, Nancy.

I pray for your safety and love for always.
All my love Forever,
Frank
P.S. I can't believe you wrote that letter. But keep it up!

After reading that letter, I am pretty sure that it had the effect that I thought it would on Frank. I really like the part of his stammering and stuttering to find words to say to me, but the main thing was it took his mind off of his surroundings and made him laugh.

The writing of the letter was also good for me. It made me smile when thinking of his reaction when I wrote it. We had gone back to playing around with each other and having fun in our letters which was an amazing feeling.

Oh, just in case you wondered, Frank had a photographic memory and I was sure he would hold me to every word I wrote him in that letter.

Frank continued to be upbeat in his next letter.

August 20, 1971
Dear Nancy,
Hi, my Darling. I love you so very much. It would be so nice to be holding you next to me and be whispering in your ear just how much I love You. I want so much to hold you in my arms and whisper to you how good I feel just having my arms around you. I want to feel you lying beside me at night, watch you peacefully and safely sleep in my arms.

I want to feel like I did when I was home on leave, I just couldn't stop smiling. I just felt so happy and contented just being with you. I've never felt that so deeply before and it really is such a good feeling. To be able to smile and not stop smiling. No matter what happens, you're able to smile at it and like it.

What a wonderful world this would be if everyone could have that feeling. We would have no need for wars or hate or animosity toward anyone.

It's not me either. I have nothing to do with this feeling. It's only my feeling it that makes it part of me. It's you, Darling. You're the reason I feel this and you're the only reason I do. You instill in me the feeling of love and trust. With these two items, I sincerely feel that I can lick the world and win.

Did you know that you're directly responsible for what I am or what I become? It's a big responsibility but in my opinion, you've not goofed yet and it's a good possibility that you won't. You're my inspiration in whatever I do. My thoughts are continually on you and what you would think.

Honey, our life was so great for two weeks, but I could tell that you were thinking of the time when I would have to go back, and I was too, still it was wonderful. So just think what it'll be this next time with nothing hanging over our heads. How alive and fresh we'll both feel. To tell you the truth, I don't know if I can wait another four months and twenty-five days. HA! HA!

How's everyone in your family doing? I hope they are all well and doing fine. Tell them all "Hi" for me and tell them to write if they get a chance. I've written my folks one time and besides that, I've only written to you. I just can't find the time. I sometimes don't have time to write you as you've probably noticed. Just tell everyone hello and that I'm still here and that I'm getting short. HA.

I'd like to make you a tape, but I can't seem to get a day off. So be patient it may be another couple of months before I get off or maybe I can when I have CQ again. How's that? OK?

Honey, I'm back on the old subject again but I can't help myself. I love you. I just love the hell out of you. I can't help it and if I could I wouldn't lift one finger to stop myself because it's too good for me. I was made to love and take care of a woman and God knows that woman, it is you. So be prepared to be taken care of. OK?

I'd better close and get ready for work. Good night and my love please take care of yourself. I love you too

much to face life without you. God bless you and our happy marriage.
All My Love Forever,
Frank
P.S. Could you send our little Instamatic over with a couple of rolls of film? Oh, and some peanut butter??? Pretty please. I love you.

That is such a beautiful letter and I am so glad that I finally received it. As I have mentioned at the beginning of this chapter, Frank had been receiving my letters, but I was not receiving his letters. I continued to write to him because I did not know what was going on. Fear was growing deep in my mind that something had happened to him. I prayed every night that God would let me receive a letter from Frank.

Finally, after over two weeks of not receiving any letters from Frank, even at the risk of it upsetting him, I wrote him a letter asking him why he was not writing to me.

August 22, 1971
Dear Nancy,
Darling, I'm sorry you think I'm not writing. Honey, I write to you every other day at least. I've been worried about you because the last letter I got was postmarked the 13th and I hadn't heard from you for a while until today. I thought you were sick or not feeling good or maybe upset with me.

I like you, only have one thing that I live for and that is you. So, your safety and wellbeing are so very important to me because it's the only way I'm assured that you're ok and that your love for me is still as strong as it was. This same principle applies to me writing to you.

A couple of times I've been later than every other day. Once I had to work twenty-four hours out of forty-eight and I was just so tired that I didn't eat anything just slept. The second time was when on the day I was supposed to write they (85th Evac. Hospital) called down to OPs and asked for a blood donor with AB+ blood.

So, they came and picked me up in an ambulance (truck) and rushed me over to the hospital to give a direct blood transfusion to a guy that was messed up pretty bad. I didn't mind because my blood gave him a chance to live. Nancy, he just kept screaming and crying for his Mom. Anyway, I was very weak, and I crashed till time to go to work again.

So, if you're not hearing from me then, I'm sorry. I'm trying to write as often as I can. I know you worry about me and I wouldn't have it any other way because it shows that you love me very much. But you should know I wouldn't do anything to intentionally make you worry. I love you too much to do that to you. This you should know.

So please don't worry so much when my letters get held up or you don't hear from me because you know I love you and I'm going to write whenever possible. OK? Ok.

Hey, Honey, I love you. How about that? Know something else? I can't stop thinking about that sweet smile of yours. You remember that last morning when we were getting ready to go to the airport and you asked me if ... and I said no we'd better not? Well by golly, I wish I had that chance again. HA! HA! Better yet, I'll take you up on that offer now. Can you arrange it? HA! Lookie there, I do have a sense of humor left.

Excuse the wet spots but it's only sweat. I'm trying to catch it on a towel but a few drops escape. Boy, it's hot over here. I finally found a tiny fan and I nailed it to the wall about six inches over my head and it keeps it fairly cool. You'll probably have to put up with me sleeping

on top of the sheets with no clothes on. But, then again maybe, I can covert you into doing the same. Whoopie!!!
 Honey, I'd best close for now and go back to work before I get fired. HA! God bless you my Darling and protect you until I'll take care of you by myself. I love you so very much and I always will. See you in 146 days.
 All My Love is Forever Yours,
 Frank
 P.S. I love you, Nancy.

The above letter was written to me on the 22nd of August and Frank had just received a letter from me dated the 13th of August. Instead of my letter taking five days to reach him, it had taken nine days. There was definitely a problem with the mail service. The only thing that I received from him was an envelope with a money order in it and a short note saying he loved me.

 I was determined to write to him every day asking him where his letters were until I received a letter from him. Frank knew that all he had to do was write me a few lines telling me he was safe. Was he hurt? Was he upset with me? Had he decided that I was not worth his love? So many questions were going through my mind and so many prayers were being said.

 At twenty-one-years-old, the only person I truly trusted was Frank. He was my everything. I had many self-doubts and insecurities at the time, but I had never felt insecure about how much Frank loved me.

 If Frank was injured and not able to write to me, I decided that if I kept writing someone would write back to me and let me know or my letters would start being returned to me. This was a terrible feeling and I was in a panic.

 In the next letter, Frank has realized that his mail was really behind in getting to me and how worried I was about him.

August 24, 1971
Dear Nancy,
I would just like to say that I love you and I believe you know how much I do. Secondly, I'm not treating you rotten. I'm really uptight and upset. Not at you but at this damn mail. I have written you at least every other day and I'll swear that to God and anybody else.

I know you worry and the only way that I may keep you from worrying is to write to you. So, name me just one reason I wouldn't write. Even if I was hurt there are lots of guys that would write to you for me and let you know what's happening. Please, for God's sake believe in me and trust me enough to know that I'll write. You should know by now that I love you as much as a man can love a woman and you should also know that with a love as strong as I have for you that I'd never do anything to hurt you or worry you.

I'm very upset. I don't even know if this letter will get to you or not. You think you're worried sick! I don't want you to be angry or upset with me, but I sure don't want it when I haven't done anything to make you this way. I can't understand how the money order got through and the letters didn't. You didn't get any letters about how I felt about the possibility of us having a kid or adopting one or about our working hard?

I realize that by the time you get this or if you get it, that my letters should have been received but I'm so upset tonight that I don't know what to do. Honey, please believe me. I love you and I pray that you already know this. You're all I have, and I love you with every ounce of life I have in my body.

Right now, our supply route is not in our hands and I don't know if mail is getting through. Although, I'm get-

ting mail from you. It doesn't make sense. I don't know, I just don't know.

Honey, I'm sorry if anything I may have written has upset you or bothered you. All my intentions are good. I just love you so much and it kills me to see this happening to you and there is nothing I can do to prevent it. I'm sorry you're having to go through this because you know that I never wanted it this way.

God, I love you so much my Darling and I always will. I pray to God that this letter will reach you and you'll understand what is going on. Believe me, I am writing and I'm not mad at you or upset because I love you and how could I be mad at the one person in life I can find no fault with?

God bless you, my love, and protect you from pain and hurt and anything else that may ever change you. Please believe in me, Nancy and believe in our love.

All my Love to you, My Darling,
Frank
P.S. I love you more and more all the time.

God's beautiful intervention was always in our lives.

August 26, 1971
Dear Nancy,

Hi! I love you so much. I got a letter from you today and you said you had gotten three of my letters. Oh, you don't know how good that makes me feel. I've been so very worried about you not receiving my mail. I'm so relieved.

God, I love you, Nancy. Believe me, I love you more than I ever thought a man could love a woman. Nancy, your letter today was the most mature that I've ever seen you. I only hope that I can be as mature as you. I pray that my happiness and that all you need is me to be happy is *true. If so everything else will be happiness plus. In other words, if all you need is me to be happy, then everything more than me that I can give you will really blow your mind. And Darling, I really want to make you the happiest woman alive.*

I love you so very much. How can I say it? I want you to feel just what I'm feeling now. I want you to really understand how I feel because that way you would know just how much I love you and need you.

Honey, I've got to close and get some rest. I'm really beat. I'm sorry this is so short but time itself is short and the _ _ _ _ _ _ _ army is trying to make 26 hours in a day and my body just isn't in that mood yet.

So good night my Darling and just remember that I'm on your side 100% and my love is the strongest thing you've ever seen or ever will see. God Bless you and keep you from harm.

All my Love is Yours,
Frank
P.S. I love you, Nancy

I am so glad that we have progressed to having real live and instant communication in the world now. It would have been so wonderful to have been able to text, Skype, and email Frank while he was in Vietnam in 1971, especially when the mail was so slow.

Of course, I say that but then I would not have these beautiful handwritten letters. I wonder if our love and faith in each other and in God were only strengthened by having to wait on each other's letters?

4

padlock and key

Letters between Frank and I were finally arriving but at a much slower pace. Some of our letters were taking over ten days to reach us and out of order. This made it hard for us to communicate but we were both trying to remain calm until we figure it all out.

The greatest thing for me was knowing that Frank was alright, even if he was a little upset with me for writing every day and asking him why he was not writing. Actually, he affirmed to me that his friends would write to me if he was hurt. Frank's buddies all knew how much we loved each other.

Frank was thinking deeply in his next letter.

August 28, 1971
Dear Nancy,
I love you so very, very much my Darling. I miss you so much. I feel like a part of me is missing. Really it is. The most important part of me was left behind. The part of me that gives my whole life meaning and purpose. Without this vital piece of me, the rest of my life is meaningless and not even worth living.

This piece or part of me that is so instrumental in my existence is my dear wife's love. With this small four-letter word rest the key to me. This key opens me. It opens me up and lets loose everything that governs the way I am and the things I accomplish or in all, it makes me, me.

Without this key, I'm like a padlock whose key is lost, I'm completely worthless. Just like a padlock is no good without that key, I'm worthless without your love. Now that I've had this love I can't do without it. I'd rather die than to ever be without it. You mean just that much to me, Darling.

> *What I'm trying to say is that I can't live without you. I love you too much to be without your love. I just love you so much, Nancy. I thank you so very much for loving me. For choosing me to give the greatest gift to.*
>
> *Nancy, I have to close for now and get some rest. I've got to be at work at 2:30 am and it's almost 10:00 pm. Please keep your wonderful love strong and whenever you get down in the dumps just remember, I love you and I always will. No matter what happens, my love will always be strong and unwavering.*
>
> *God bless you and take care of you for me. I love you so.*
>
> *All my Love for only You,*
> *Frank*
> *P.S. I love you X 1,000,000,000,000,000,000,000, 000,00 = how much I love you.*

The letter above is such a special letter. Frank had a beautiful way of thinking about his love for me and putting that love into words that became engraved on my heart for eternity. He always thought that he could not express his love for me with a pen on paper but there is no doubt that he definitely could and did.

The next letter is really a short letter, but Frank knew how much I worried about him and with the letters being so slow and erratic, he wrote to let me know that he was okay.

> *August 30, 1971*
> *Dear Nancy,*
> *Hello Honey. I love you. I'm sorry that this letter has to be short but I'm so tired. I'm fighting off sleep now. These 12x12's are killing me.*
>
> *Lee is leaving tomorrow. I really feel great for him. We're getting short, you know? Well, we are, and I can*

hardly wait. Honey, I long to see you and hold you so much. Our time is coming if we can just be patient.

Honey, I'm sorry, I really am but I have to close. I know this isn't much, but it'll let you know that everything's okay and I'm alright. I'll write you a long letter tomorrow afternoon, I promise.

Please be careful and keep loving me as you always have. God bless you, my Darling.

All My Love,
Frank

Frank mentioned to me in the above letter that Lee was leaving the next day. Lee was Frank's roommate and best friend. I detected from Frank's mention in his letter that he was very happy for Lee to get to go home but a little depressed at losing him to talk to. They were like brothers.

The mail was not all getting through. I am not sure how many letters are still out there in La La Land. There is absolutely no way to know if Frank and I received all of each other's letters.

Frank had written to me early about letters being taken then used to send spouse's fake reports of their soldier's deaths or capture. In the next letter, he is very worried about the letters that are missing from his footlocker, which he had received from me.

August 31, 1971
Dear Nancy,
Well, Hi there Honey. How's this day find my wonderful, beautiful, and loving wife? Wow! How was that? I hope it was alright because those three adjectives are among the many, many that fit my feelings toward you to a tee. I think the one term that sums all these up is

the one word, love. That small word means so much and says so much. In our case, it means everything

Last night, I promised to write more tonight. So, here I am writing. I'd like to apologize for last night's letter again. I was just dead, and I hope you'll understand. I wrote because I hadn't written the day before and I know you worry, so that's why I wrote.

Lee left today, and I sure hated seeing him go. I loved that guy like a brother. He was one of the best friends I ever had. I'm going to miss having him around but I'm very happy to see him able to get out early. He hated this Army as much as I do and I'm glad to see him getting out.

Hey, you keep asking about that form from the airlines. Didn't you get my letter of about three weeks ago telling you that someone threw that away? I wrote you and told you about it. The form was lying on a footlocker in one of your letters and the next afternoon both were gone. Apparently, someone threw them away.

Something's happening to my letters. You don't seem to be getting all of them. I'm sorry Honey but I have no way of knowing if you're getting all my letters or not except by your letters.

Guess what? I already ordered your birthday presents. I ordered them early because I want them to get there on time. Promise me that you won't open them until your birthday. I know your curiosity is stronger than you but please fight it just this once.

Tell you what, why don't you take the packages, when they come in over to your folk's house or to mine and have them put them up till your birthday. I want to surprise you for once, please. And the answer is no, I won't tell you what's in them. HA! HA!

If you get me anything expensive, I'll shoot you. Really now, Honey, we can't afford expensive gifts and still have a honeymoon in California and still be able to live comfortably afterward. You know you don't have to prove your love to me. That's one thing I'm very confident in. Just get me a card and write "I love you" on the inside and I'll be happy. Very happy.

Honey, I love you so much. Just thinking about you gives me such a wonderful warm feeling. When I get out I'm going to make you the happiest and most loved woman in the world. My goal in life is to bring you happiness and joy. I love hearing you laugh and enjoy yourself. It makes me feel so good to know you're happy.

Honey, I live for you and you alone. What more can I say? You're just my entire life and it's such a wonderful life having you as my wife. I love you. I love you. I love you.

I've got to close now. I get so wound up trying to convey so much more feeling to you than I can write down. Please, Please, take care of yourself for me, Darling. I pray for you and for our love to be everlasting. God bless you, my love. I love you so very much.

All of my Love to my Wife,
Frank
P.S. I love you, Nancy.

From the letter above it is quite obvious that I never received all of his mail.

Frank is very upset at the end of this next letter. He starts off okay then his mood changes drastically. He is not feeling well. They did not have balanced meals to eat and most of the time there was little water to drink. There was probably a bigger abundance of beer than water.

When I got this letter, I was extremely worried about him. I'll just let you read it for yourself.

> September 3, 1971
> Dear Nancy,
> I love you, Darling, with every breath I take or every thought I think, you're there. I'd rather feel this depressed feeling and this awful loneliness that is almost continually surrounding me than never have known the wonder of loving you.
> Nancy, you've given me the greatest gift that life has. You've given me yourself. Wholly and completely. I could ask for nothing more from you. You've given me everything that you possibly could and believe me, Darling, I treasure your gift and I could never ever want for more. Just sharing your life is more than enough for me.
> If you could just imagine how much I love you, Nancy. I just can't live without our love and my love is nothing if you aren't there loving me. Just knowing that you're back in the world waiting and loving me means everything to me. Just keep loving me and never doubt my love for you because it's the strongest part of me and I guarantee that nothing can defeat it or make it weak.
> I've been so frustrated the past three days. I just wanted to tear something up. I'm so uptight inside. I'm sorry I'm so upset but my nerves are shot, and my temper is too short. I've changed so much since I've gotten back. This place is not nice anymore. We're living like animals. The shitter is about five feet from my hooch and the mud, rain, and everything else.
> I'm not easy going anymore. I fight at the drop of a hat. I've been passing blood in my stools for a couple of weeks now and it hurts like hell. I want to get the hell out

of here and become a human again. Seems like I'm nothing but a mess of problems, huh? I'm not. Everything's ok. I'm just tired and mad about stupid stuff.

Only 134 days to go. I'm sorry, I've used some words I've said and I'm sorry I dropped all my problems on you. I'm just not myself at times and I look for something to lean on and you're the only person I can open up to. You're more concerned and considerate about me and my feelings than anyone in the world.

I feel so much older and grown-up than others my age and I married a mature woman who's been through so much hell and trials and still, she has faith and strength to carry on. I don't believe other women could take what you've taken and still stand by their husbands' side and be ready to take more.

You're the greatest, Nancy and I love you so very much. Nancy don't pay any attention to my complaining about this place because I'm rather depressed and I say things I don't mean to say. Please love me and keep me forever in your heart because you're all that I have and all that I'd ever want.

God bless you, my Darling and I'll be seeing you soon. All my love is yours, Nancy, if you want it and even if you don't, it still belongs to only you.

And Love will Conquer all,

Frank

P.S. Smile for me. Can you? I see it. I'm smiling now for you because I can see you and feel your love for me just glowing

This letter was very shattering to me. Frank was so depressed and sick. Also, his best friend, Lee had left.

We had known Lee in Okinawa and it was very comforting for me to know that he was there with Frank. I knew that Lee would let me know, as soon as he could if something happened to Frank, but now I did not know the soldiers around Frank.

Something was going on over there and I did not know what it was. The mail had gotten twice as slow or not getting out or getting totally lost. I prayed that God would go and help Frank. Frank was my heart and soul, I could not and would not lose him.

5

disposition form letter

I was very worried about Frank and knew his last letter to me was so out of character for him. Frank seemed to have lost all of his inward fight to depression. I prayed that God would touch Frank with His loving hands, pull him out of the depths of depression and mend his body.

The next letter Frank typed on a *Disposition Form*. It shows his resilience and God's hand in answering my prayers. I will try to put it in here as much like the original as I can.

DISPOSITION FORM
Subject: My love for my wife!!!!!!!!!!
To: My wife, Nancy
From: Her husband, me
Date: 05 September 1971
Dear Nancy,

Hi!!!!! Amazing isn't it? I can really type. I am on C.Q. The last goof up was the typewriter, not me. I had to rewind the ribbon. Hey, did I tell you yet that I love you? Well, if I haven't then I am sorry because I really do. You can bet I do! More than anything in this world, I love you. How about that?

Right now, it is raining like a son-of-a-gun. About 400 inches a minute. Boy, this typewriter is different from any I have ever used. I guess I will get the hang of it soon. So, be patient.

Honey, I am really sorry for what I wrote the other night. I was just tired and did not feel really well. So, I ask you to forgive it. Sometimes a person says things that he or she does not really mean when they are depressed or upset. I hope you will understand.

Things are really not as bad as I sounded. I mean this is Vietnam and things are expected to be bad but sometimes, I just get to feeling sorry for myself and I lean on you. I am sorry if anything upset you or caused you any concern. This was not intended. I just felt sorry for myself and I needed a shoulder to cry on and you were the closest. Please forgive me for acting like a fool.

    I am really sorry, and I ask you to please forgive me. I realize that you have enough to worry about without me burdening you down with my troubles and feelings. So, once again I will say that I am sorry. Beyond that, all I can say is that I love you so very, very much. Hey, enough of my saying I am sorry. I love you more than anything in this world and that is all that should count.

DISPOSITION FORM Page 2
Subject: Continuation of my love for my wife
To: The same old wonderful wife
From: The same old hubby
Date: same old 05 September 1971

    Yep, I made another page. Wow! Hey, kid, did you know that I love "you" so very much. Boy, "you" did not come out very right did it?? Well, I am working on it. ha! ha! Even the ha ha's did not come out. Well, I never claimed to be a "secetary", now did I? Besides that, I can't even spell, "secatary" (secratary), right can I???

    How is everything on the home front? I hope that everything is ok with you. Other than that, I just don't care one way or the other, like I have said many times, "you are the only thing that makes life worth living." Believe me that, that is exactly what I mean too.

    My life would not be worth living without you and I really mean it. I guess, you just have to face it, I love you and there is nothing you can do about it. Like it or not, woman, you are stuck with me and the only way out is to stop loving me and I know your love is too strong to let this happen. So, it looks like we are stuck with each other forever. Heck, that does not sound too bad to me. Ha! Ha!...

I haven't heard from you in three days and I only hope that you aren't sick or under the weather. I also hope that I haven't done anything to make you mad or upset with me. If I have then I am sorry, for anything that I may have done that has upset you. I only try to think of your feelings and if I have hurt them I want you to know that this was the last thing on my mind.

DEPOSITION FORM Page 3
Subject: continued (my love for my wife)
To: The most lovable wife in the world
From: The Hubby
Date: 05 September 1971

I love you too much for me to do anything that would hurt you and you of all people should know this and understand.

Hey Honey, I just realized that two days ago was my Dad's birthday. I did not even get a card or write. This really makes me feel low. I did not even know it was September until I found out today I had CQ. Time means nothing except for the days. I never know what day of the week it is or anything.

I hope you mentioned to him on his birthday that I wished him a Happy Birthday. Gosh, I really feel bad. The only dates I remember is your birthday, my birthday and May the 8th. Other than that, the days are just one of a number that has to pass before I see you again. Please tell him that I am sorry, and I just plain forgot. I will try and explain to him when I get a chance to write them.

Hey, could you send me our old Kodak? I would like to get some pictures over here before I left. Another thing I need is a picture of you. A recent one that shows your (mine) long hair. I found another picture frame and all I need is another picture. So, if you could, please send me one.

Well, I've just been rattling on, haven't I? Well, I guess I had better close for now and get back to CQing. I have just one more favor to ask. Could you, pretty, pretty please with sugar on it send me a tape????????? I would just love to hear your voice.

Well, I guess I had better close. God bless you my love and keep watch over you for me. YOU KNOW I LOVE YOU!!!!

All my love now and forever,
Frank
P.S. I love you and miss you!

That was such a fun letter from Frank. He was worried about being so open to me in his letter from September 3rd. I think Frank was afraid that he had let me see weakness in him and was afraid it would turn me away or cause me to love him less. What Frank did not know was that his total openness in showing me his weaknesses only endeared him to my heart more deeply. I loved this man and I knew this man's heart and soul. What he had really done by opening up this deeply, was to let me in past his feelings of manhood into his real fears and insecurities making us deeper into being one soul.

In the next letter, Frank solved the mystery of the extra slow mail.

September 07, 1971
Dear Nancy,
Hello Darling, I hope this day finds you well, happy, and cool. It's hotter here than 14 stoves. Pretty hot, huh?

Well, it was 114° at 10:00 am this morning and God knows what now.

I got two letters from you today, one from Gram and one from the Okie (Okinawan)Credit Union. I hit the jackpot, didn't I? You'll have to excuse my writing because I'm writing without support and I'm trying to catch my sweat before it gets on the paper.

Your two letters today really perked me up and made me happy. You're great, you know it? You can take me when I'm in the worst mood and make me happy and smiling. You're just too good to me. I only hope I can repay you for all the joy you have given me.

You mentioned being mad at yourself for worrying about my not writing. Don't be. I worry when I don't hear from you. It's just natural. I'll explain why it probably took so long. The V.C. had the only road out of here. We couldn't get any supplies or anything. Once and a while a truck got out and in but for about a couple of weeks, it was pretty shaky.

I didn't want to tell you cause it would, I felt, worry you too much and you had enough worries of your own. The situation has been relieved, and everything is ok now. So maybe this will explain why it was a long time before you heard from me. OK? OK.

As far as making a fool of yourself in my eyes, bull. Could I make a fool of myself in your eyes? I hope not. Whatever you do or say, you have a reason for doing so and I think I'm mature enough to understand it or try to anyway.

You ask if I wanted you to go back to work or not? Well, you seem to me that you're looking for me to make a decision. Well, first off, I don't know enough about it?

DISPOSITION FORM LETTER

Are you bored? Do you want to work? Are you happy not working? Is the time passing slow not working?

I'll give you my opinion. I don't want you to work if you don't want to. The most important thing is your happiness. You want to get these tests run and I feel that this is more important than a job. If I was there and could see how you felt I would say, "No, you're not going to work". I don't want to say no if you really want to work. So, I'll say no, and you take it from there. If you really and I mean really want to do it, do it. Alright? Alright. You see, I'm behind you in anything you want to do.

Hey, nut. Yea, you. I think you're crazy but that only means that you're like me, so fine. We'll go bananas together. HA! HA! You asked what else could I expect from a perfect wife? Well, I expect you to get over here in two more days. A perfect wife fulfills all her husband's needs and you haven't fulfilled my needs for about a month and a half. So, if you want to keep that perfect wife rating then you'd better hurry up or I'll demote you to a near perfect wife. HA! HA!

I guess you couldn't tell I miss you, now, could you? You said you were going to iron tomorrow. Well, I'd almost be willing to bet a month's pay that you didn't make it. Be honest. HA!

You said don't be surprised if you pop into my dreams. What's keeping you? I'm more than ready for you. I love you!! And I will be here waiting for you!!! Well, soon we will unleash all of our pent-up desires for each other and we'll probably heat up the whole town of San Francisco. HA! HA!

In about a week we'll only have four months or less left. I say less because about November the 1st, if I haven't heard anything about Christmas drops, then this kid is going all the way to the top just a screaming and hollering all the way. So, keep your fingers crossed.

Hey, I'd better close because this is getting to be a book. So, I'll say adios and I'll see you about 10:00 pm in my dreams. You'd better show up or I'll have to fly into your dreams and I have to be back by 2:30 am. HA! HA!

Seriously, Nancy, I love you with all my heart and soul. Please take care of yourself and keep loving me. God bless you, my love.

All my Love forever,
Frank
P.S. 10:00 pm sharp now. I'll even shave my face for you. HA! HA! I LOVE YOU, LOU!

Finally, we were back to having fun and kidding with each other in our letters. It was so good to be receiving letters in a timelier way. Frank knew that I disliked ironing but did it one item at a time, as needed.

Frank knew I was faithfully writing, and I knew he was too. Letters were our only way to communicate. I cannot imagine how hard it was back hundreds of years before the Vietnam War.

Frank was still upbeat in his next letter.

September 10, 1971
Dear Nancy,
Well, how's my wife today. I almost said lover, but I don't think that would be the correct term. After all, to be lovers you have to sleep together, and I don't know if you've noticed it, but lately, we haven't exactly been sleeping together for a while now. I've noticed it. HA!

I guess you can tell that I'm a little crazy tonight. Well, it's better than being depressed and upset. So, I'm looney!

Well, I'm back. Didn't even know I left, did you? Well, I did for about thirty minutes. It was my turn to make the beer run. So, I'm back Big Deal, huh? Well, anyway, here I am. Ya, miss me?

My nose is running like a fire hydrant. I think I'm allergic to Vietnam. As a member of the medical profession, I prescribe a long rest in a dry climate like Texas, plenty of good food, and lots of bodacious, wonderful, good loving.

I know that in Van Vleck they have a rest home for weary soldiers that have freckles and beer guts. It's run by a good looking, sexy, love-starved woman. So, would you mind making me a reservation?

Honey, it's getting dark and as old and feeble as my eyes are I can't see in the dark. So, I'll have to say goodnight and take care of yourself. Because I'm going to be there for that reservation soon.

God bless you, Nancy and I pray for him to take care of you because you're everything to me and my existence depends on you.

All my Love for You Forever,
Frank

Frank has told me nearly all that was going on, but he has not mentioned one thing that I had not forgotten about. In his next letter, he will finally write to me and give me an answer to one question I had been asking him.

September 12, 1971
Dear Nancy,
I got four letters from you and it was great. I love you so much.

Hey, Honey, it may be a while till you hear from me again. I've had serious hemorrhoids for about a month now and today it was just too much to stand. So tomorrow I'm going on sick-call and getting something done about them.

I don't know if they'll put me in the hospital right away or if I'll have to wait. So, if they put me in tomorrow it could be a couple of days until one of my buddies can bring me writing paper and such.

Now it's nothing to worry about. I just wanted you to know so you won't worry if you don't hear from me for a couple of days. OK? OK!

I read in your letter that you were at your Grandmother's house. How is she? Tell her, I said "Hi" and save me some of those pecans.

Honey, I hope you're alright. I worry about you so much. I want to make you very happy when I get out. You've suffered enough and now it's time for us to be happy and enjoy each other.

You mentioned that drive to your Grandmother's house and how we talk. I really did enjoy that maybe the most and I'm glad we both share the same interests and like doing the same things.

I'm lonely, Nancy. But soon I won't be. We'll talk for hours and hours.

Honey, I have to go and eat before they quit feeding. God bless you, my love. I love you with all my heart and I always will.

All my Love for You,
Frank

While Frank was home on leave, we had driven to my Grandmother's house which is a six-hour drive from Van Vleck. We took our time driving, stopping along the way for a picnic and really talked to each other. We made many plans on that car trip for our future when Frank got out of the Army. We shared our thoughts and dreams with each other. We had really missed these talks with each other.

Finally, Frank had told me what was actually going on with his health. Was I worried? You bet I was but all I could do was wait until I heard from him again.

If you remember back to before Frank went to Vietnam, he volunteered to go to Vietnam, so others with small children and pregnant wives would not have to go. Frank was not a "Fortunate Son," nor did he ever ask to be; even with migraines and bleeding hemorrhoids, he would stay till his time to come home. Frank was an honorable man and always did the right thing.

6

man's love not a weakness

THE LOVE STORY OF NANCY & FRANK

I did not receive a letter from Frank for four days and was really worried about him. In his last letter, Frank had told me that he would be requesting a sick call to see about getting something done for his severe hemorrhoids. He was not sure what could be done or when. All I could do was pray for him and wait to hear from him in a letter.

Of course, Frank and I knew that he would not be a priority at the hospital in Phu Bai, Vietnam. Phu Bai had a hospital called the 85th Evacuation hospital but it was for soldiers wounded in the field, evacuated by helicopter, stabilized, and sent to a bigger hospital in Japan for more intense treatment. Frank had given a direct blood transfusion to one of those soldiers, so he would never have asked to be a priority.

Frank's next letter says something that I truly believe all men should read and apply in their lives.

September 16, 1971
Dear Nancy,
Well, hello there. How's my Darling doing?
Honey, today I'm really lonely. I miss you so very much. Here I am a grown man fully capable of taking care of myself and my needs. So, why does my whole life depend on you? Why does everything I do say or think have you in mind?
I may be able to take care of myself but without you're love, Nancy, I'm not worth taking care of. What I'm trying to say is that I need you. I more than need you, I've got to have you. I don't like having to say this, but you have me sewn up.
The reason I hate to say it is because a man doesn't want to be weak and he sure doesn't like to admit his weakness. But my love for you is no weakness as long as your love for me stays there. It's my strength. The only

way it can ever become a weakness is if your love for me goes sour and then life isn't worth living anyway. I guess you could say your love is to me what spinach is to Popeye.

Hey, did you make it through the storm okay? We got some pictures of Sinton in yesterday's paper and it really looked bad. I hope everything is alright.

Honey, I'm in a weird mood tonight. I want to tell you just how much I love you and I can't with this pen and paper. I'm going to try and get a tape off to you as soon as I can. I'd love to have one from you if you could, please?

I'm going to close for now and go to bed. I need you to kick me in the pants and tell me to quit feeling sorry for myself. So, I guess I'll have to do it myself. Ouch! I forgot about my hemorrhoids. HA!

God bless you, my love, and know in your heart that I love you very much.

All my Love Forever,
Frank
P.S. I'm about ready for a "dream date" any time you're ready.

Frank did not give me any information in the above letter about what was going on with his health situation. The only clue I had was the fact that he was feeling really lonely which made me think they had put him in the hospital.

I had gone to my grandmother's house for a few days because we had a hurricane coming into the Gulf of Mexico which did damage in Sinton, Texas. As soon as the threat was gone I came quickly back to Van Vleck. I wrote to Frank every day while I was gone but did not receive mail from him until I got home.

THE LOVE STORY OF NANCY & FRANK

The letter is really beautiful as he discusses telling me how much he loves me, and it was not a weakness for a man to tell a woman that he loved her. I loved that my love for Frank gave him strength because his love for me gave me that same strength. He was my Popeye and I was his Olive Oyl.

Frank's writing in his letters for the last two letters is very calm and seems to flow effortlessly across the pages. He really seems to be more relaxed.

September 20, 1971
Dearest Nancy,
I love you. In a hundred and seventeen days, you and I once again will be as one. That is what we were both made for and that is what we both want. The ability to live together as a couple, as a partnership and a family isn't easily obtained. Yet, we two have accomplished this feat with relative ease. Why? Well, I feel it is because we are so deeply in love and so very compatible with each other.

Look up the divorce rate in our country. So, that fact right there should show you how hard it is to find true compatibility and happiness while living with a member of the opposite sex. It's hard for me to understand because, for me and yourself, it was so easy.

I believe the reason it's easy for us is because we understand each other very well. But the biggest factor is that small overused word, love. Many people use it too lightly. When I use the word love it explains an emotional, physical, and psychosocially feeling.

It explains everything that is happening to me at once. It describes how I feel, think and hurt, and all these feelings are directed totally to you. To put in simpler terms, you own my heart, body, and mind. You are the sole possessor of me. In other words, I'm yours for as long as you can stand it.

I'm making you a tape. I did half of it today and day after tomorrow, I'll finish it up and send it to you. I just remembered something. I hope you remember it too. I didn't get to write to you for a few days, but I explained it all in my tape, so I won't go into it again.

I'm really looking forward to seeing you again. I guess that sounds crazy but I am. I really am going crazy to see you again. It won't be long now. Here we are sliding down the hill and getting closer and closer to the bottom.

What a happy day it will be when I walk out of the Army and into my love's arms forever. I'll be the happiest man in the world. I love you so much my, Darling. We're going to be so very happy again. How good it will feel to know that it is permanent, not for thirty days or whatever.

To know that I'll never be more than a few feet away from you at any time. To know that when I'm lonely all I have to do is call and you'll come running into my arms. To sit down over a quiet cup of coffee and talk. To feel your warm body laying tenderly close to mine. To wake up in the morning and see you so peaceful in contented sleep. I can go on and on forever.

It all amounts to the fact that, Darling, I love you with all my heart and I need you by my side for all times.

I have to go now, Hon and get some much-needed sleep. Take care of yourself and I'll be there soon.

All my Love for all my Life,
Frank

From the above letter and a cassette Frank sent to me, I know that the Doctors figure out a way to fix his hemorrhoids to help him get well.

There was one problem, Frank being in the Army Security Agency and his security clearance. Putting Frank to sleep during a surgery meant another person with his same security clearance had to be in the room with him. I do not know if they put him to sleep or not.

Frank sent me a tape telling me all about this, but I do not have the tape. All I have are these letters and he does not go into any detail about what happened.

> September 22, 1971
> Dear Nancy,
> A happy day to you. How's my woman today? If your love for me is as strong as my love for you is then everything is alright.
>
> Here, I am on my three days R&R. I couldn't afford to go to the R&R center at Da Nang, so I'll spend it in my room writing you and reading. Just to have three whole days off from work to relax is going to be fine. It also gives me time to be alone and think. To make plans for when I get out.
>
> I got your letter about going to your Granddad's place when I get out. I'm glad, I really am. In California, we wouldn't be really alone. There would be people all around and I'm greedy. I want you all to myself. I don't want to talk, see, or listen to anyone but you. I want all your attention. In short, I don't want to share any of you with anyone.
>
> I've done without all of you for so long and now I will not, and I mean will not do without you anymore. I've paid my price for the free world, our economy, South

Vietnam, and our government. Now, all I want in return is about two weeks with my wife in solitude. If that's too much to ask then too damn bad because I'm going to get it.

Maybe this doesn't sound like old easy going me. Well, it isn't. I've been pushed and told what to do when to do it, and where to do it long enough. In 115 days, I'm going to start getting my way and get the things we both want. It's our turn.

I want this to be a closely guarded secret. I don't want people to know that I'm home. I don't want anyone knowing where we are. I will not tolerate people breaking our peace. Maybe you think I'm being a fanatic about this, but I want this very much and I'm looking so forward to it that I don't want it spoiled by anyone.

If anyone wants to know why you're meeting me in Houston, then tell them that I'm meeting you then we're driving to Louisiana for a second Honeymoon. I'll meet you in Houston. I want you to register in a hotel there near the airport and I'll come to the hotel when I get there. We'll work all the details out later. Without you, nothing would be worth anything for me.

Honey, I'd better close for now. My heart is beating 100 miles an hour just thinking of seeing you again. Take care of yourself and remember me in your prayers. I love you and you know I do. God bless you, my life.

All My Love,
Frank
P.S. IIICO DREAMING!!!!

Frank definitely need this three-day R&R to recover, heal, and just relax.

My granddad's place was a farm up in the Hill Country about sixty-five miles Northwest of Waco outside of a little town called Fairy, Texas. The house sits back off the road on a hilltop and you can see for miles. Frank and I loved this farm and the peacefulness that emanated from it.

In Frank's next letter he was really excited and also answers some of my questions.

September 25, 1971
Dear Nancy,
Hi! I love you!! I got five, yes five letters from you today. I'm just sitting on top of the world. I sat down and read every one of them in complete excitement. Weird huh? No, just thrilled at hearing from you and reading how much I love you and you love me.

You say we're getting "short". Well, you're right but we're not getting short enough. Pretty soon though, I'll be fighting my way to Oakland then into the great "state" and into the great arms of my Wife!!! "Aurk"!! That's "Argg", I just misspelled it.

I wrote my folks two days ago. So that solves the promise you wanted me to make.

I don't believe it!!! Your fingernails are growing!!! Eureka!!! What's the matter?? You put poison on them or what?? Looks like our next fight is going to be a really good one, huh? HA! I know you plan on doing a job on my back, huh? HA! HA! Feel free to do so by all means. HA!

What's this hip language? "Decent", "Out of sight"? You're getting hip, huh? Well, you'd better not get too hippie, or I'll have you running around the block till you get less hippie. Joke! HA! HA! Well, so what!

MAN'S LOVE NOT A WEAKNESS

Now for the serious side. You were worried about a kid in Hue getting killed over a watch. It's bad and I'll admit that, but it's expected. You'd have to be here and see the stuff that goes on before you can understand it.

I don't really blame the guy. He shouldn't have killed him though. That sounds cruel, doesn't it? Well, you know me, and you know I don't get violent easily. So, take it from there.

You're right about him being in trouble. Funny thing though you don't hear of a kid getting in trouble when he throws a grenade in a jeep and kills three Americans. No, he's only a child. Well, I tell you what, children over here kills people.

It's the wrong way to feel but you can't help it. My whole goal is to put my time in, go home, and get there just like I left. With all my body parts. So, you get this way and like I said it's wrong and that's why I want to get out of here because I don't like feeling this way. I'm sorry if you disagree with me and think less of me for being this way. I really am sorry.

You say you don't care if I come home naked, "as a matter of fact, I'm looking forward to having you home and keeping you that way." Well, Honey, I want you to remember you said that. Because I'm really looking forward to it. I love you.

Honey, I'm going to close for now. I'm so happy and I'm getting "up tight" (more hip talk) because I can't convey how I feel.
I'M HAPPY AND I'M IN LOVE!!!!!!!
God bless you, my love and I'll see you in 112 days.
All My Love for You, Forever,
Frank
I LOVE YOU

THE LOVE STORY OF NANCY & FRANK

These four letters from Frank cover so many feelings from him, from his feeling that a man does not show weakness by telling a woman how much he loves her, to Frank really wanting to get out of Vietnam and stop having feelings that he knows are cruel and wrong. Like Frank wrote, children over there killed people during the Vietnam War.

7

guard duty & thoughts on war

Our letters were arriving from each other in the time frame that Frank and I had become accustomed to. Thank God, the doctors had managed to get Frank back to becoming a healthy soldier and he had been on an R&R which gave him time to heal and relax a little. Finally, we were coming to the end of September, 1971. We were both doing the best we could to make the days go by faster and praying that Frank would get an early drop to be home for Christmas.

The next letter I got from Frank caused me to worry.

September 27, 1971
Dear Nancy,
Hello, my Darling. How's the most precious thing in the world, today?

Honey this letter has to be short. The lights are out and I'm doing this by a candle. It's doing a job on my eyes.

I got your letter yesterday saying you had ironed. Well, you sure are getting it together. Every letter you seem to be getting more and more excited about my coming home. This is making me get excited too. I can hardly wait.

I love you in good spirits. It perks me up and keeps me going. I just love you so much.

Honey, I'm going to close for now. I'm sorry this is so short, but I'll get a longer one off soon, I promise. Please take care of yourself and keep that love for me going.

All My Love is Yours,
Frank

No lights, what did that mean. I was not sure, but I was definitely worried. Candlelight meant that light was permitted.

Frank would not write to me for three more days and I really worried about him until I got another letter. It seemed like there was never a true moment in this time of not worrying.

You have read enough of Frank's letters by now to know him and you will read, as I read that he was being very evasive in the next letter, too.

September 30, 1971
Dearest Nancy,
Well, today brings to close another month. Another thirty days seen, met and beaten. I always love to see payday come. Not because of the money but it brings another thirty days to a close.

It's really hard to believe that I have 107 days left. It seems like I was born in this army. There for a while, it was looking bad but now I'm starting to feel short. It's a good feeling, it really is.

Hey, have you gotten your birthday gifts yet? I hope they got there in time. I ordered them on the 25th of August, so they would get there in time.

The old world is going to be so beautiful when we're together again. All the love we have had to keep inside so long will just flow out of our hearts. I'll hold you so long that you will probably think you're my Siamese twin. But that's ok with me. I don't want you out of my sight for more than a couple of minutes. I love you so very much Nancy.

Are you sending me a tape? I hope so. It would be really nice to hear your voice again.

Honey, I'm going to close. I realize my letters aren't very long but there's nothing to say except, I love you. I spend all my time thinking of our life after we put this

Army behind us. So when I try and write it seems to lack so much in revealing my thoughts and emotions. So forgive me for writing such short letters.

Please take care of yourself and pray for our day. I love you, Nancy.

All My Love,
Frank

Frank was beginning to feel very depressed again. It was close to his birthday and to mine. Since married, we had never been separated for so many important dates to us. Frank and I had not missed our Anniversary or birthday together since we married but in 1971 we would be separated from each other for both special occasions.

In the next letter, Frank talked to me about how he felt about the war, about a disappointment he had experienced, and why he was feeling so depressed. In this letter, you will actually get to experience how he talks to me through his written words as if I was right there by his side.

October 3, 1971
Dear Nancy,
I hope this letter finds you well and in good spirits.
I am sitting out in the boonies about 300 feet up in a tower. It would be quite beautiful if I couldn't see the choppers, armor, and the tools of war in general. The hills and countryside would be really nice to gaze at if it weren't for the twisted dead trees, the shell holes, and the smoke rising from them.

You know, I have sat down many times and tried to figure out just what wars are for. It doesn't make sense for things it took God thousands of years to build and make beautiful to be destroyed in fifteen minutes by the hands of man.

You know yourself, I am very much for my country and I will support it in any way I can. But I also am for nature and living till I'm old and of no use to mankind anymore. I also understand that some wars have a good purpose, but I only wished that men would sit down and talk out their differences instead of fighting them out.

I don't know what the answer is. I'm so fed up and disgusted with this Army and so tired of seeing it run by a bunch of people who don't value human lives (as long as it isn't theirs) and care only about money and prestige.

I don't know why I talk about such things. I only do it when I'm so depressed or down in the dumps. I'm sorry if I bored you with my carrying on or made you depressed. I'm going to get this depression off my chest now if you don't mind.

It all started yesterday when a guy I know on swings came in who has 5 days less than I do toward ETS. His original ETS was in January. Mine was dropped from February to January because that's my DEROS date (Date Estimated Return from Overseas).

Well, he came in and said, "Hey guess how many days I got?" So, I said five less than me or 100 DLITA (Days Left In The Army). He said, "Nope 10 DLITA (Days Left In The Army). He told me that a message came in giving everyone ETSing in November, December, and January 90-day drops.

God, I was so excited. That means I would have been home in 15 days. So, I ran over to personnel to see if my name was on the list to get a drop. I knew it was, but I wanted to make sure. Well, it wasn't, and the reason is my original ETS date is February.

So tough luck fella. I should have known better than to really expect it, but I did anyway. So, therefore, I got really depressed. It looks as though we're going to have to spend our full 104 days, Honey. Ok!

Alright, let's get to some pleasant talk, huh? Ok! Have you got my tape yet? I hope so. I'm still looking for mine.

Well, I'm back. Boy, that's a long climb. A dude brought me out some c-rations. So, I've dined. Ugh! Chicken and Noodle, crackers, peanut butter, a can of peaches, and some Kent cigarettes. Some meal, huh?

Oh well, soon my beautiful wife will make me some of her famous macaroni, cheese, and meat. You know, I've been thinking about that for about two weeks now. When I'm really hungry, I can see all the pies and food you used to make for me. I just drool all over myself.

But what I think about the most is just you. How soft you are, how wonderful your voice sounds, how good I feel when you call my name or say I love you, how soft your eyes are when you're looking at me, how soft your hair is and how long it's going to be when I get home, how your body looks and feels, how your mouth tastes, how your mouth looks when you smile, how delicate your hands look, and the sound of your laughter.

There are a million things I think about when I think of you, Darling. I miss you so terribly. Promise me you'll never leave my side when we're together again. I want you near me as often as I can have you there. Your undying love for me is the dearest thing in the world.

I've been constantly thinking of that week or so that we're going to spend alone and the thought of it just makes me happy. Because "You make me so very happy. I'm so glad you came into my life." Remember where that come from? Blood, Sweat, and Tears #1. It's a good song. It says what I feel.

Hey, did you ever get your birthday gifts yet? You haven't said anything about them yet. I sure hope they got there on time. How does it feel to be 22? I don't feel any different. Next birthday kid, you had better be ready because this guy is going to treat you to the biggest night on the town you ever saw.

Honey, I had better close while I can still get this in an envelope. Excuse my depression but telling it to you has helped me shake it off. Thanks for listening and I hope I didn't upset you. There's no need to worry about it (as I have just realized) because it won't do any good.

So, put your chin up and smile for me, Ok? OK! One more time, please. All my love will always be yours. God bless you, my Darling.

All My Love for You,
Frank
P.S. I LOVE YOU

The above letter made me cry when I first read it and it makes me cry every time

I read it. Not just because of how disappointed and depressed that Frank was but also for his deep expression of love for me through his descriptive words of me.

Frank's words make me feel like the most loved woman in the world then and forever. He had memorized everything about me as I had about him. Those memories of each other would never fade, no matter the length of separation.

I remember where every freckle was on his body, the sound of his laughter, his beautiful amber eyes when he looked at me softly with love in his eyes, his soft tender kiss, his arms holding me warmly, safely, and securely, the way he whispered softly into my ear telling me how much he loved me and those big dimples that melted my heart and soul with just a glance forever.

In Frank's next letter he will tell you what he is doing on his twenty-second birthday and his humor melted my heart. Frank had the ability to shrug depression off of his shoulders and face each day as a new day.

> *October 4, 1971*
> *Dear Nancy,*
> *Good day to you. Here once again to bring you the excitement, adventure, and fun of war. From high atop the lush mountains and valley of the A Shau Valley, we will bring you once again the daily life of a man who is defending his country and its way of life and loving every minute of it.*
>
> *As our story opens, Sp/5 Henderson is keeping a wary eye open for commies, who could very well at this moment be sneaking through the head high elephant grass. From his tower, he can see for many miles and is constantly on the alert for enemy action. With his trusty M-16, 43,000 full clips of ammo, flack vest, helmet, radio, comic books, cot, c-rations, flares, pen and paper, and canteen, he is at constant readiness for any possible aggressor.*
>
> *Suddenly, he hears his call sign on the radio. Base defense calling! He answers, "Roger Gunsmith control. This is gunsmith kilo, over". No reply! Have they (commies) intercepted my call? He tries again! No control! Are we being attacked?*
>
> *Then a thought pops in his head. Batteries. But, of course, his batteries are dead. Another crisis avoided by this quick thinking, ever vigilant, guardian of our freedom.*

Exciting? Had you on the edge of your chair, huh? HA! HA! HA! Boy, I'm weird, aren't I? I even laugh at my own weirdness.

You know talking out my troubles to you yesterday, really helped me over a very depressing period. I said to myself, what the hell's the matter with you, boy? You've got more right now than you've ever deserved.

I have you, Nancy and you're a lot more than I'll ever deserve. So, why should I get so depressed? I know you're waiting for me and you really love me, and I love you so much, so what is the matter with being happy? So once again, I'm splitting my freckled faced mug with a smile instead of a frown. OK? Ok!

Shocking isn't it? Getting two letters in a row, huh? I've got the time and I feel good because I'm so much in love and so much loved. I love you so much even if you love me only for my body. HA! HA!

I'm anxious to get back to my hootch tonight, so I can see if I got any mail. I get in too late to pick mine up, so I got a buddy to do it for me today. I look so forward to your letters. It really boosts the old morale up. I like to read where you love me and see where you're excited about me coming home. It reflects the same feelings I have.

I can't wait to take your hand and go walk and exploring through the woods together. Better yet. I can't wait to rip your clothes off and smother myself in your warm soft flesh. Now that wasn't nice, was it? HA! HA! HA!

I guess I've gone on enough. So, take care Honey and keep looking ahead. God bless you, my love.

All My Love,
Frank
P.S. I love you, Nancy

Frank was back to accepting what was happening in our lives and it was good to see him being humorous again. We were one and we would not be discouraged but we would spend our time of separation writing to each other, encouraging each other, and telling each other how much we loved each other.

God was our strength and He was seeing us through all things while loving us and making us a complete one heart and one soul forever.

8

poem to my wife

We had a little disappointment when Frank's name was not on the list for an early drop but we knew that each day that passed would still get us closer to being together again. Also, we knew that no matter how many days we had left of separation nothing could change the deep love we had for each other.

Frank had turned twenty-two years old and spent his birthday in a guard tower overlooking the A Shau Valley. The devastation of the valley that Frank saw looking down from that tower brought out deep thoughts about the Vietnam War and war in general which he shared with me in a letter.

When I received Frank's letter, it was as if I could see with his eyes what he had seen. Frank appreciated the beauty of God's creations in this world. I remember when we were in Okinawa watching Frank climb the cliffs, stand on top of the highest one for a long time, and stare out across the China Sea as if he was taking all of the beauty into his memory never to forget. While Frank would stand there peacefully lost in the absorption of the beauty in front of him, I would stand by his side watching his face taking a picture into my memory forever of him smiling and standing there appreciating the work of the hands of God.

Frank's was really happy and excited in his next letter.

October 7, 1971 6:30 am
Dear Nancy,
Good Morning Darling. It's 6:30 am in the morning here. We got a hum-dinger of a typhoon coming. Edith. What a name! Anyway, after work yesterday, we spent the afternoon in the rain putting sand-bags on our roofs and picking up trash that might blow. These people worry too much. It was then still 400 miles from here.

> It's expected to hit Phu Bai about 2:00 am in the morning of the 10th.
>
> I got your package on the 4th. Perfect timing. I'd been down in the dumps but seeing that someone really thought of me made me realize how stupid I was. Thank you so very much my, Darling, for everything. I got two cards from you, one from my folks, and one from Gram the next day.
>
> You don't know how happy you make me, Darling. Not with the gifts or cards but with the thoughts I know are behind them. You don't realize how wonderful it is to know that you're back home and 100% behind me and are in favor of me and proud of what I am or what I do. It gives my whole life purpose and meaning.
>
> You're the greatest person in the world. I Love You So Much!!!!! Honey, I hope your birthday was happy and I hope my card and gifts got there on time. You deserve the best and I only can hope that you get it.
>
> Honey, I'm going to have to close. I just got through working from 3:00 pm to 6:15 am and I'm on my chow break so I have to go back and work my regular eight-hour shift.
>
> Be good and remember, I love you with every part of me. May God bless you and take care of you for me.
>
> All My Love to My Only Love,
> Frank
> P.S. Hico here we come!!!!

I received my birthday gifts from Frank the day before my birthday. I had promised Frank not to open them until my birthday, so I kept that promise to him.

Frank sent me a beautiful wooden jewelry box. The jewelry box is fifteen inches tall, thirteen inches wide, and eight inches deep. It has five drawers that are lined with maroon velvet. Some of the drawers have divisions and some do not. Frank also sent me a pair of jade post earrings which came in a silk pouch with a snap closure on the front of it. I treasure these gifts from Frank and will forever.

Frank wrote me another letter dated the same as the above letter but at 8:20 pm at night. He was on C.Q. so he typed the letter. This letter had a very special poem in it written by Frank to me.

> *October 7, 1971, 8:20 pm*
> *Dear Nancy,*
> *Hello there my beautiful Wife. How's every little thing with you today? I hope you are in good spirits and are feeling well. Because I love you and I want you well and feeling happy. I command you to be happy. That is a direct order. Ha! Ha!*
>
> *I guess you can tell, I am on C.Q. tonight. Why you may ask because where else would I get a typewriter? Well, I am, and it is about 8:20 pm at night and I am just sitting here and typing you a letter. My typing may not be very well, but I thought it would be different for a change.*
>
> *I got a picture of you today and I must say I don't like it. It doesn't show you very well. You are too far off in the distance for me to get a good look at you? How about letting your hair down and getting a close up of you? Pretty Please.*
>
> *Now don't misunderstand me I liked the picture, but I want one that shows your face and the rest of you more. The predominant part of the other picture is the couch and the room and to tell you the truth, I am not really interested in the couch or the room.*

I have a color picture of the Frank, but my buddy is in it and he doesn't have any pants on, so I think I will wait to send you one of another kind. It would not be so bad, but he does not have any clothes on at all but his shirt. I at least had my shorts on. Ha! Ha!

That mean old nasty typhoon looks like it is going to miss old Phu Bai after all. We are still getting rain and other mess of a typhoon but the typhoon itself is not going to hit us. I am going to change paper because I do not know how much paper I have left in this machine, so hang on tight while I roll.

Wow! Just in time, huh? You remember that jar of peanut butter you sent me in my package? Well, I was naughty, and I ate all of it last night. Boy, I am a pig! I just got started and all those crunchy peanuts and the first thing I knew it was all gone. I did not mean to, really but I could not stop myself. I feel just like a kid who got his hand caught in the cookie jar.

Well, I guess you will just have to punish me when I get home and make me stay in bed for at least three days. Of course, I will need someone with me to watch me and make sure I don't sneak out and be naughty again (I'm not mentioning anything about not being naughty in bed). Ha! Ha! You see, I'm being naughty already.

I guess I was just born to be naughty. Ha! Ha! But I've got a sneaky feeling that you do not really mind. Go on admit it. Do not be bashful. You are not blushing, are you? You had better be.

Gosh, I am in a good mood tonight. About time, huh? Well, I really feel pretty good because I just realized that in 100 days, 3 hours, and 15 minutes, I will be free and at home with my woman again. Hey! That's 99 days, 3 hours, and 15 minutes. Boy, I can't even count. Yep, in

3 hours and 15 minutes, we will be two-digit midgets. About time, huh? I hope you're keeping that love light burning.

I sure am letting my emotions flow out tonight, aren't I? Seven or more days off in the woods with me alone? Are you sure you are up to it? Ha! Ha! Well, it is time to roll again I think so as 1. You figure out what as 1 is yet? It means (in 05h language) wait 1 minute. Cool, huh?

Hey, be sure and tell Jimmy, he owes me a Swisher sweet cigar and a free drunk. You seem to be so happy for them and I am too. I hope they are very happy, but I imagine they are. Tell Jimmy to change a few diapers for me and not to get his hands dirty. Ha! Ha! I trust your folks are well and all in good health.

They seem to think they can make me work 24 hours today and I don't know if the kid can make it all night again tonight. This typewriter is cool, and I think I may be a professional typist when I get out. I am good enough, aren't I? Ha! Ha! So, I can't type so good, but I still love you anyway. Just because you maybe can out type me, I don't hold a grudge, as long as I can hold you while you type.

We get off of 12 & 12 in two days. Yippee!!!!!! I am so tired of working 12 hours a day and waking up at 2:30 am in the morning.

Here I am after a break of about two hours. Some of my buddies came over and kept me company for a couple of hours. We just sat around and drank some beer and talked. They went to see "Vampire Lovers" tonight at the outdoor flick. I have been waiting for weeks to see that flick and it looks like I have missed it. They said it was really bloody.

POEM TO MY WIFE

    I can't wait to get home and lie on the floor and watch the movies together like we did when I was last home. I really enjoyed that very much. Just the little things we did, I seem to appreciate the most. The times when we could just be alone and be ourselves.

    Sometimes I think we are crazy but we both seem to enjoy what we do, so who cares. When I get home this time, I want both of us to not play any games and just say and do whatever we feel like doing. To completely relax and be ourselves and know that we don't have to impress anyone or try and appear as we think we should. We both know each other and know what each other are like so we should really be able to relax and love life as we both need to do and enjoy doing.

    I am really looking forward to being with just you again and loving you the way you deserve to be loved. Loving you from 10,000 miles away is not what you deserve. It is not what I deserve either. We were made to live with each other not miles apart. We are part of a very wonderful life and to complete this life we have to have each other and be able to see and hold each other and talk to each other at all times.

    Our love is so strong when we are apart, just think of its potential when we are together again. We are just liable to burst apart from the joy and happiness. Oh, Honey, I love you so much and I long for you to be by my side so much that I can't even think straight. I challenge anyone to love a woman as much as I love you. It can't be done.

    Honey, I guess I had better close for now before I write a book. You know that my love, faithfulness, and my devotion are yours for all time and forever after. I pray that God will look after you and keep you safe till I can once again look after you and take care of you myself.

No matter how low you feel at times just remember that your husband and lover cares for you more than anything in this old world and that no matter how bad things seem at the time they will pass, and I will do my best to give you the best life possible because that is exactly what I feel you deserve.

Take care my, Darling and pray for me as I do you and keep loving me like you always have.

All My Love to my Wife, Nancy,
Frank

P.S. Have you checked out your Grandfathers farm and made sure we can use it and that no one will know?????

My Poem to My Wife, Nancy
This is meant for my wonderful wife,
whose very presence has added meaning to my life.
For what would have happened to this poor fool,
if it were not for the deep clear pool
of pure, honest, beautiful love and devotion?
The world's greatest feeling and emotion,
which keeps me alive and going strong
for as long is long.
She has all my respect and admiration
and my life is to grant her every possible consideration.
Although we are separated by ever so far,
we will not ever show a mar.
There is only one woman for this man
and she is the most wonderful in any land.
Any fool can see who she must be,
it's my own sweet wife, Nancy.

POEM TO MY WIFE

I may not be good with words or verses, but I only hope this in some way shows you my great love and respect for the woman I call my own.
I love you, Nancy so very much.
Frank

I love this poem and it is the very first poem that Frank wrote for me, but it was not the last.

Frank was a very special man, a man who thought deeply, a man who knew how to love deeply, and a man who knew how to express his love to me at all times. God blessed me with Frank. You wanna be loved like that and you wanna love like that.

9

love explained

The poem Frank had written for me made me cry as I read it over and over. I put the poem and his letter back into the envelope, I walked to the cedar chest at the end of our bed then placed the letter into a white box which was inside it. After shutting the lid on the cedar chest, I set propped up with some pillows on our bed then wrote him a letter.

This white box inside the cedar chest which held all of the letters I had received from Frank while he was in Vietnam in 1971 would forty-seven years later be opened by me again only after it was revealed in a dream for me to look inside this cedar chest. This white box of letters would become a priceless treasure full of letters of Frank's eternal love for me.

In Frank's next letter he is eating homemade cookies and talking seriously to me about love. The box I mailed to him for his birthday held homemade cookies which he loved.

October 9, 1971

Dear Nancy,

I bet you don't know just how good these cookies taste, do you? Well, let an expert tell you. They taste delicious. I have been eating them this morning and I'm about to finish them up. I guess you're wondering why I'm writing so much. Well, between guard duty, CQ, and my day off (today), I've had a lot of time to myself and I can't think of anyone who I would rather spend my time with.

I'm sitting here with some water boiling in an old coffee can for my OD green coffee (instant) and eating cookies and smoking. I wrote my folks and your folks the other night on CQ after I wrote you.

Hey you. I love you. I hope that you know how sincere my love for you is. I also hope you know how true and devoted my love for you is. It's really hard to explain my feelings for you, Darling. What I think it amounts to is I have turned all my feelings, emotions, and mind to you and this is all yours now. You have made a gift of all these things to me also.

We give all the feelings or love to each other reluctantly at first and each one of us held back a little of ourselves because we were afraid to completely trust each other with the greatest gift one person can give another. Slowly we began to see that this gift we were partially giving was also being offered in return.

So, little by little we started giving a little more and a little more because we found that we were trustworthy and that we also got the same amount back. Now, we are over the cautious period and we both pour everything that we have into our love and this is what really makes our love have the beauty it now has. We were cheating each other but in the back of our minds we had to be sure and by gosh now I have no doubts and I never will again.

I knew all along how much you really loved me, but I was afraid to be totally open to you. I knew you doubted me and now I can see where you would. I never showed my love in the ways I should, I never spoke of love to you, and in all, I treated you rather bad.

This separation has been hell but from my viewpoint, I really am glad it happened. It woke in me the feelings I had been trying to hide and not let take over me completely. It has made me realize that I love you more than anything in this world. It made me realize that I'm so very lucky. It has made me realize just how important it is for me to show exactly what I feel and tell you what's in my heart and what I feel for you.

I used to think if I showed you how I really felt you would take advantage of me and think of me less of a man. I thought you would think I was weak and not as a man should be. I know now that a man can be open and show his feelings and still be a strong man and respected too. You haven't treated me any different, quite the contrary, now you are more open, and I feel you love me more than ever.

So, I made my mistake and I hope you'll forgive "my" stupid maleness that possessed me for so long. I will admit that the way I acted was the part of a fool and thank God, I realized my mistake and corrected it before I broke your heart or hurt you any more than I already had.

Our life is beautiful now because we both are open in our love and above all, we are honest and truthful with each other. Now that I see how wonderful our love now is, I can't see how I could have been so blind for so long. I guess it's just that I was never mature. I feel now that we both have reached more maturity and oh how beautiful it is!

I explain all this to you because I feel you understand me better than anyone else. I want you to understand that you have everything I have and it's all yours and always will be. I want you to know that nothing is being held back from you or will it ever be. In other words, I love you, my Darling with a love greater than any man could ever love a woman.

When I get home you'll never find another more devoted husband, lover, and father. Yes, father. We are going to have a kid. With a love as great and wonderful, it's impossible not to. I'm serious. We are there now. We are both being totally open and truly in love and we will never part again. I feel now God will give us a child. So that's all there is to it.

Darling, I'm going to close for now. I want you to understand that anything you want from me is yours. I will do anything in my power for you and all I want back is your love. God bless you my Darling and keep happy because you can bet when I get home, I am going to make you the happiest woman in the world.

My life is devoted to making you happy and secure. Take care of yourself and pray for me and our love as I do.

All My Love for You and You Alone,
Frank

Every time I looked into Frank's beautiful amber eyes, I could see how much he loved me and I know he knew how much I loved him.

I think the letter above has one of the best messages about love in the marriage of two people. We fall in love and in the beginning, there is a true passion for one another then we start the daily adjustment to each other's habits, mood, and thoughts. Next comes the battle of learning to really give and take with each other which is the blending of two individuals in becoming one.

Trusting, understanding, being open, and forgiving each other in marriage are so necessary. No one wants to have their heart broken by the one they truly love but without true trust, openness, understanding, and forgiveness in a marriage or a relationship you can never truly open your heart to one another.

Once you totally open up your heart to each other your love will soar into a beautiful dimension without boundaries and you will become one heart and soul entwined together as one strong thread.

Frank and I really loved each other from the very beginning but we loved each other so much that we were afraid to totally be vulnerable to each other for fear of being heartbroken. Being totally reliable on each other away from all family had bound Frank and me together quickly and had already begun the steady trust in each other.

Frank was so right, the separation we were going through quickly broke down all our walls of fear of being totally open with each other.

Extraordinary circumstances of war and separation crashed our walls down to dust instantly and both of us openly threw our emotions out to each other through letters and cassette tapes. We realized that it really didn't matter if our hearts got broken because we had to let each other know how deeply we loved each other.

What I am trying to tell you is, openly speak your love to your spouse or significant other. A hug and a kiss are awesome but the spoken words, "I love you," "I need you," are priceless. What are you waiting for? It's never too late. Do it now.

Frank carried a piece of paper in his billfold at all times. This piece of paper had a beautiful saying on it.

If you love something, you will not be afraid to set it free.
If it comes back, it is yours.
If not, it was never meant to be.

I believe if you love somebody, don't be afraid to tell them. If they don't reciprocate your love, then they were not your person, but your person is out there looking for you. Go find them.

The next letter Frank wrote is very confusing for me. I do not have any letters between the above letter dated October 10, 1971, until this letter dated October 15, 1971.

Frank had been so happy in his last few letters and this is why this letter is confusing to me. I do not know if he was upset with himself for not writing for a few days or just upset again about not getting a drop. I am sure that others who had received the drops are leaving which was a continual loss of close friends. Also, he was very worried and thinking about our future once he was out of the Army. I just do not know.

October 15, 1971
Dear Nancy,
Well, I guess by now you realize how much of an ass you married. I guess I'm just crazy. I don't really know what's wrong with me at all.

I just have trouble believing that everything is going to work out so fine. I know it is but I just don't want to believe it because I'm afraid if I do it won't work. I'm really mixed up.

If you can just put up with me for 92 more days then I think I'll be ok. These last few months are really dragging me down. I keep thinking about getting a job, going back to school, and all the other stuff. I think and worry about these things because I don't want to fail.

I keep wondering if I can do it. I want to so much. I want to do everything right, so you'll be proud of me and trust in me. I'm looking forward to it because it's a test of my abilities. In my ability to take care of you and raise and care for our family.

Also, I'm kind of scared of failure too. I have always enjoyed a test, the chance to compete, and I'm usually fairly confident in myself. Yet, I have never entered a competition as strong as this. All I'm asking of you is your confidence in me and to stand by me with all the love you have. I'll do the rest.

When I get these feelings sometimes I don't really know. One minute, I have all the confidence in the world, the next I don't have any. I'm like I said before, mixed up. That's why I feel the week or two we spend up there alone and completely by ourselves will do us both so much good.

We can completely relax and let all this tension and built up pressures out by strictly being at ease and being completely happy. Pretty soon you can actually forget how it is to feel depressed and lonely. Loneliness has to be the worst feeling in the entire human feeing system. I don't ever want to feel lonely again.

Right now, I'm putting everything else aside and just looking for enough ahead to see getting out and spending two weeks with you by ourselves. Then we can make our plans and decide on what we're going to do. We'll have plenty of time to sit down and talk. I picture us sitting side by side by a small creek or stream or even on the side of a hill and talking for hours.

I'm sorry, I'm such a bore and I'm so damned weird Honey. I know it's asking a lot to put up with me but that's exactly what I'm doing, is asking you to stay by me and my foolishness for 92 more days and then I'll try to explain my feeling and try in some way to make things up to you if I can.

I love you and no matter how stupid I seem, my love for you isn't. You're the only thing in this world that means anything to me anymore. I can't make it without you and that beautiful love of yours. I'm sorry once again.

God bless you, my Darling and keep you safe for me. I love you, Darling.

All my Love is Yours,
Frank
P.S. Could you kick me in the butt?

LOVE EXPLAINED

When I decided to write this memoir, the above letter was the deciding factor in where this memoir would end. Originally, I had decided to end it with the last letter I received from Frank from Vietnam, but this letter spoke to me. Frank was so worried about what he would do after getting out of the Army and since I knew what extraordinary things that he actually did after his discharge from the Army, the Memoir could not end with the letters.

There was one thing that I knew for sure and that was whatever Frank decided to do, I would always be so proud of him, standing by his side, holding his hand tightly in mine, and loving him with all of my heart. He owned my heart and soul and still does.

Please don't forget to speak your love openly whether you are a man or a woman.

10

dearest fancy

Frank was really worried about our future in his last letter. Even though he was getting upset and depressed, after a few days of thinking deeply, I knew Frank would come back with the strength that was in him, realize how much I loved him, how proud I was of him, and together as a team, we would work out the future. The next letter proves how resilient Frank was.

>October 17, 1971
>Dear Nancy,
>Dearest Fancy, huh? Well, I'm in a fancy mood tonight. Are you over the shock yet? Yep, old grouchy nasty me is in a fairly decent mood. No, I'm not feeling sorry for myself and brooding. I'm just as lonely as I was a few days ago but I've wised up a little. I hope! Sometimes I can really be a dick, can't I? Well, I've had my little fit for this month and I bet you're getting kind of tired of them aren't you?
>Well, as the saying goes, "being in love means never having to say you're sorry". Well, I believe in that even though I don't practice it. I feel you understand me and know I have my moods and you love me, so you accept them even though you don't like it. You don't get angry because my weird moods are a part of me and you love me.
>See now, I've thought all about these things that I'm too ignorant to realize when I get in one of my funky moods. If I can learn to think of these things when I'm like that, then my stupid tongue would keep still or better yet, my writing hand would write LOVE instead of depression.

Yep, the kid has got his confidence and ambition back. Once again, I can lick the world and every S.O.B. in it but I had to get my head on straight. TIMEOUT.

Ok, TIME IN. I had to make me a cup of that good old OD Green coffee. Ugh! Oh well, what the heck. Surprised you, didn't I? You thought I was going to say hell, didn't you? Well, see what a good boy, I am? Well, most of the time I am.

Well, we finally got off of 12 & 12s but getting a day off is still like trying to swim home. Now, I'm not knocking trying to swim home because if I get much hornier, I'll try it and make it if I can find water deep enough where I don't drag bottom. Maybe, I can pole vault over the ocean. Good grief, Frank!!! Oh well, I figure you know how I feel. We'll just have to do something about that when our time comes.

The more I think about it, I feel we should spend maybe three weeks at your Granddad's farm. Or better yet, a month. Better than that, let's just stay there forever and be alone. The more I think about it, the better I feel and the more anxious I become. I'm really excited about it.

You know what I think about a lot? Of seeing you for the first time again. To see you smile and maybe a little tear in the corner of your eye when you see me again and me trying to act cool and not just split my face wide with a simile and never succeeding. Then I'll walk out the gate and you'll be in my arms and by golly, I don't care if the whole city of Houston is there, I'm going to grab you and kiss you for at least thirty minutes. People will just have to go around you and me cause I'm not moving until I have you in my arms and taste your sweet lips.

I think then I'll let out the biggest happiest yell you ever heard and tell everyone I see I'm out of the _ _ _ _ _ _ _ army, I'm in love and I'm the happiest S.O.B. you'll ever see. I can hardly wait. I'm so happy just thinking about it. I love you so very much!!!

Wow! Here I am on the 3rd page! What's come over me? I really feel like writing tonight. I've been thinking about writing you all day and I really enjoy sitting down and talking to you. This is the closest I can get to being with you and it's a good feeling.

I got your letters (three) yesterday. I'm glad you're helping Connie and Jimmy. It sounds like they really appreciate your help too. I bet Jimmy is running around like a chicken with his head cut off. HA!

What things are you going to do for me? No surprises. Yea surprise me. I've been racking my brain trying to figure out just what these surprises are. Don't tell me, Ok?

You said you were sorry about not remembering the microphone for my tape. I'll quote you then chew you out. "I'm sorry, Honey, I should have some sense by now and know how to remember things, but I don't, but I promise if you'll keep loving me as you do now that I'll try to make up for all of my dumb faults."

Alright now. Here it comes. "If I'll keep loving you." Bite your tongue. Have you ever thought that I could stop? I couldn't. Not ever. So, you get that dumb thought out of your head right now. Next, I don't care if you forget my name, but don't you ever forget that you love me, and I love you. That's the most important thing. "I'll try to make up for all my dumb faults." Listen as far as I'm concerned, your only fault is putting up with this dumb ox for so long.

If you don't quit cutting yourself down you're going to be in trouble. I love you and I love you for what you are. All these things you consider as faults are what make you what you are. That's part of you and if you ever change one little thing about yourself, I'll be disappointed. The clicking sound you make when you're asleep, crying at sad movies, your laugh, your smile, your tenderness, and so many other things are all you and they are what makes you, Nancy.

I love that Nancy and I like her just the way she is, and I wouldn't trade one of these things for anything in the world. So, you stay the way you are because you're loved for being yourself and being the only Nancy like you in the world and this man is so very happy to be the man in your life. I love you, Nancy and that's all there is to it.

Darling, I have to close before I write a book. Please take care of yourself and keep that love you have for me going like it always has. I couldn't ask for anything more. God bless you my wife and keep you safe for me.

All my love is forever yours,
Frank
P.S. Tell your Dad that I'm getting ribbed about the Texas vs Okie game. I can't stand it and I hope your Mom is putting it to him also.

Frank never failed to get himself together, get back to being positive, and look ahead to coming home. He was a fighter and would not allow his emotions to get the best of him, ever. He kept me positive, lifted my spirits, and taught me how to dig deep inside myself to overcome all obstacles.

A year is a very long time to be away from the person you love. The feeling of the length of that separation has never left me. It is a feeling that you cannot put into words.

Frank's next letter is a short one, but his spirits are high.

> *October 19, 1971*
> *Dearest Nancy,*
> *Hello, there my Darling. How's my life today? I hope you are in as good spirits as I am.*
> *I'm getting short. We're going to be with each other soon. Oh, happy days, years, and just one hugely happy lifetime.*
> *I received two letters from you yesterday and one today. They were great! Maybe you think your letter writing doesn't mean so much because you can't express yourself, but Honey, your letters mean so much to me!*
> *Your letters make me so very happy because I can read of your love for me and how happy my love seems to make you. I love you so very much.*
> *Honey, it's late and I really must go to bed. I know this is short, but I'll get a longer one off tomorrow. It's been a long rough day. Please take care of yourself because you're the whole world to me and I'm worthless without you.*
> *God bless you and keep you safe.*
> *All my love for my darling, Nancy,*
> *Frank*
> *P.S. Tell everyone "Hi" and I will see them all soon.*

Around the first week in October, I had gone to Killeen, Texas, to help my sister-in-law, Connie, and my brother, Jimmy, with their newly born daughter who was the first born niece for Frank and me. She was so precious, and it was so much fun to be asked to go with them to their home and help out with the baby.

I do not remember how long I stayed with them, but it was an awesome experience. I had written to Frank to tell him where I was. He thought maybe I was glad to get away from our little white framed house, but I missed it.

October 22, 1971
Dearest Nancy,
Well, here I am again talking to my most wonderful wife. I hope that you're doing alright and that you're looking forward to my homecoming. I'm on break today. That's why I didn't write last night because now I have all day to write.

I'm going to answer some of your questions and make a few comments then I'll check mail at noon and if I got some more mail I'll do the same again. I realize that this is late, but if you're like me there are questions I would like to have the answers to even if they are late. So, here goes.

You say that you would be more than glad to get back to Van Vleck because you missed our little house and the things you could be doing there. That sounds so good to me. For a while there I thought that maybe you were getting tired of our house and I was hoping you weren't because all my thoughts are directed around you and our house.

I guess it's because that's our first real house. It's not our first house but it's our first one in the "world". I'm kind of a sentimental nut but I love thinking about sitting on the floor late at night watching the late show together. Things like that are really pleasant thoughts.

I like hearing that you're caught up in getting things ready for us when we're together again. It will make your time go by fast and it makes me realize that you're crazy. But not crazy, crazy but crazy about me, and that is beautiful.

I'm glad your birthday gifts got home, finally. I'm sorry they didn't get there on time, but I ordered them in August. I hope you like what I got you because I tried to get what I thought you would like. That about covers it. So, if I get some more letters at noon, I'll read and answer the questions too.

Right now, I'm listening to the Carpenters. The tape is playing "Close to You". It's really nice. That song "We've Only Just Begun" is us. It describes us so well. It's true. We have only just begun. We have so many years of happiness and love left that we have only begun to feel all we are going to feel. But it's so great now, isn't it? Just think what it's going to be in twenty or thirty years, twenty or thirty times better.

I wish that every man and woman alive could find the love that we have. It's so beautiful. I've just begun to love you too!

I've got so many questions to ask about our plans for Hico. First, have you got the keys and are you sure it's alright for us to be there? What are you going to tell your family? Will you be able to pack and meet me in Houston without anyone knowing? How about writing me and telling me what you have planned, so I can share in the excitement. Ok? Ok!

I still don't know what I'm going to tell my folks. What I'm hoping for is a Christmas drop. I went to Personnel yesterday and they said that there were rumors of Christmas drops and that maybe they would come down soon. So, keep your fingers crossed. If they do then you'll be the only one to know. So, that way no one will expect me home early and we'll have no problem. I don't expect any anyway.

If they don't like it, well I'm sorry but that's the way it goes. I'm taking that time with you and I don't care who says what. We both deserve it and by golly, we're going to have it.

Guess what? I put in for my ETS orders yesterday. That really makes me feel like I'm getting short.

Honey have you had the test run? You mentioned something about it a while back, but you've said no more about it in a long time. So, please keep me informed. Ok? Ok! Well, I'm going to knock off awhile and check mail so hold on I'll be back soon.

Well, here I am back but I didn't get any mail, so I'll have to just rap about other things. How about talking about SEX? No, that's not a good subject. It's alright when you can have visual aids to help you learn. HA! Who needs to learn? I just need a lot more practice. HA! I guess you can't tell that I'm a little (?) horny, could you?

Well, it's clouding up and should be raining in a few minutes. I'm about sick of this darn rain. I'll be glad to see old Texas and her dryness again.

Honey, do you realize that in only 86 days or less we'll be holding each other again? It seems like such a short time, compared with the 365 days we started out with. Well, it's about our turn at last. It's going to be so wonderful because we've waited for so long for it to come.

Our love has developed into something that is more beautiful than anything else in the world. We've grown up so much in these past three years and so many months. We've found the true meaning of love and happiness at last.

There is no greater feeling in the world than loving and being loved. It has its sad times but the happiness it provides more than makes up for any bad times. I'm so lonely at times I could almost cry, but never have I wished I wasn't so much in love. I wouldn't trade being *in love for anything in any world. I just love you so much my Darling. I love you so much.*

Honey, I had better close for now and try and get a shower before the water is cut off again. Please take care of yourself. I pray for God to protect you and to keep you safe for me. Keep smiling for me. Ok? Ok!

All my Love is Yours,
Frank

I do not think there is anything that can be added to Frank's letter. He was really hoping for a Christmas drop but he was also excited about getting his ETS orders put in which meant he was getting shorter.

Frank and I had only 86 days left of being separated. I received the next letter on October the 30th. It is a very short letter, but it made me dance around the room, smiling from ear to ear, and so very happy!

October 25, 1971
Dearest Nancy,
33 DLITA
"SHORT"
DROPS MAKE IT!!!
Frank
P.S. F.T.A.

This letter still makes me smile, want to dance, and shout to the world! Not 83 days left in Vietnam but dropped to 33 days. By the time I got the above letter, Frank would only have 28 days left in Vietnam. I thanked God for that over and over.

We've only just begun.

11

wife of a shorty

Frank was coming home, not in eighty-three days, but in thirty-three. After receiving the letter telling me of Frank getting a drop of fifty days, I called everybody to tell them that he would be coming home soon.

Excitement and happiness totally overwhelmed me.

I received a letter from Frank the next day and he was so overwhelmed, happy, and excited too.

> October 26, 1971
> Dearest Nancy,
> I love you! You had better get your stuff together woman. Big daddy will be there most rickety tick! That's right. That letter you got yesterday was no lie. We have 32 days left in this _ _ _ _ _ _ _ army. Not 82 but 32.
> I got a note at work yesterday from personnel and it said for me to go by there. So, I went and by God, they asked me if I wanted a drop. Stupid, huh! "Hell yes", I want a drop. So, presto you'll have your big old teddy bear home 50 days earlier. Decent!! Boy, this army is alright!!!
> Go ahead and tell anyone you want about it. I'm going to write my folks and tell them that you are going to meet me in Houston and we're taking a second Honeymoon instead of meeting in California. That way we'll be honest and truthful. So, tell anyone but don't tell anyone where we are going.
> I'm so happy, Nancy!! I love you so much and the thought that I'll be seeing you in one month is terrific. I'm so excited, Darling!!!
> I got a tape from you today but haven't had the chance to listen to it yet. I just don't know what to say. I'm so damned happy about everything. I even went and got a haircut today!! To think that by the time you get

this letter and write me back about it, we'll only have 22 DLITA is too much. I must be dreaming.

No more loneliness, no more sleepless nights, and no more depressions. Everything is going to be just great!!! I love you!!!!!!!!!!!!!!!!!!!!!!! Honey, I have to close for now because I'm too excited to write any more.

God, please take care of you for me because I'm not there to watch after you and take care of you myself. But I'll be there soon. Please take care of yourself because we've come too far for anything to happen now.

All my Love to my Darling,
Frank
P.S. Think "short"!

The letter above is absolutely priceless to me. While typing this letter into this chapter, I smiled the whole time because I could see the excitement in Frank's writing. His words practically leap off of the paper with excitement at me as I read them.

We were actually getting so close to the end of our separation from each other. It had been a long ten months but now we only had one month and a couple of days to go until Frank would be out of the Army, back in the states, and into my waiting arms again.

Frank continued to write letters to me with the robustness of his excitement.

October 27, 1971
Dear Nancy,
Well, how does it feel to be the wife of a shorty? Feel good, huh? Well, it feels good to be the husband of a shorty! In fact, it feels wonderful to be getting really short. I can hardly stand it!

I even went out yesterday and got a haircut! Of course, it was flipping up over my collar, but I did it on my own. Amazing, huh? Well, I only got a tiny bit cut off but still! I'm on the last letter of my short sheet. I colored in the 31 on the M which was the last one on that letter. Now it's only the Big E with 30 days left.

I'm once again listening to the Carpenters. It's nice. It's raining like all get out outside and it's pouring in our room faster than we can bail it out, but you know what? I don't even care. Because in 30 days, I'll be at home and looking at you and I'll never again have that empty feeling inside. No more long nights. Just happiness. I've waited a long time for this and I know that you have waited the same amount of time.

Honey, we are finally going to have each other as we both have dreamed and waited patiently for. I can't even get mad at anything anymore. Not the zips, the rain, the beggars, or the frustrations of my job. I laugh them off and say to myself, "to hell with it, in 30 days I'll be holding you and then all this war and Army will be forgotten". It's a good feeling to let everything slide off after fighting it for so long.

I don't know exactly what day I'll be home but stay by our phone the 26th and 27th of November, if possible. I have to go to Da Nang for four days then to Oakland. I don't know how long I'll be at Oakland, but I've heard at least one day. So, I can't tell you when exactly I'll be there, but it shouldn't be later than November 27th or early the 28th.

Will, that give you enough time? If not, tough stuff! HA! HA!

I got two letters yesterday and the first one I felt really bad about. It was about the letter I wrote when I was *really depressed and said things that I didn't mean and shouldn't have said. You thought I didn't love you anymore. I'm sorry if that's the impression you got because we both know better but once again my dumbness brought you unhappiness that you shouldn't have felt.*

The next letter I got you had understood and it made me feel a little better. You said you had had a test run and your tubes aren't blocked. I'm glad. You seemed to be relieved and that makes me happy too. Tell that doc to hurry up. HA! HA!

I haven't shaved in three days and until we get some water, I'm not going to. Oh well! I just thought I'd say that for lack of something better to say. I should close but I feel like talking to you, so I'll ramble on about anything if you don't mind.

I've put on about ten more pounds since I got back. I hope you don't mind. I was going to lose it my last 90 days but now I don't know if I have enough time. If you think it's too much I'll lose it and fast. I don't want you to be disappointed in me in any way. So, say the word.

My suntan is almost gone. This rain doesn't give me much chance for some sun. Honey, it seems I keep coming back to the same subject, but I can't help it. We'll be together in only 30 days. I can't believe it. I'm so happy, Darling. I love you so much!

Well, now I have to close. Please take care of yourself and keep me in your thoughts. God bless you my love and take care of you for me. I love you, Nancy.

All my love is yours, my Darling,
Frank
P.S. THINK "short"

Frank was getting letters from me about a letter he had written when he was so depressed. The mail was so slow, and it really was not fair to either one of us. We could be in the best mood and then receive a letter that was a reaction to another letter written ten days or more before. We had come to realize that this would happen, but it especially seems unfair to Frank at this particular time because he was celebrating some amazing news of a drop.

I have not received Frank's letter about the drop yet and he knew this. He is not letting my letters upset him and I thank God for that. Frank keeps writing and his excitement and happiness stay high.

October 28, 1971
Dear Nancy,
How does this day find you? Shocked? Three letters in a row? What's come over this nut, huh?

Well, I listened to your tape today and I feel like such an ass. I want to tell you one more time just how sorry I am and to try and reassure you that I could never stop loving you or ever, ever doubt your love, you know these things, I hope, but I feel so bad about the tape.

God, woman don't you know how much you mean to me. I know you do but I hope that in some way this will help reassure you and make you feel secure until I can be by your side then there will be no doubts or fears. This, I promise you.

Come on now and smile for me. After all, what do we have to be sad about now? We got it almost licked and nothing can stop us now.

In your tape, you said you had a feeling, I would be home by Christmas and maybe Thanksgiving. Well, you, smarty you. I can't wait to get your first letter back after you find out about our drop. I was so happy, and I just know you will be too.

I'd best close and get some sleep. For some reason, I have trouble sleeping at night. I wonder why? HA! God bless you my love and keep you safe.

All my love for an eternity,
Frank

Frank was trying so hard to reassure me how much he loved me but he knew that my letters and the cassette tape were old news from me. I had already written him a letter explaining to him that I understood his depression letter. It is a truly loving man who will keep apologizing and reassuring even though he knows he has already been forgiven.

In the next letter, Frank is still waiting for a letter from me letting him know that I know about the drop.

November 2, 1971
Dearest Nancy,

Good Morning my wife. How do you feel on such a wonderful day? I hope you are in as good of spirits as I am. We're going to be together very soon. That's enough to make me happy.

I haven't written to you in about three days, as I guess you realize. The reason? Well, even though I am getting short the army still thinks I should work my rear end off, so there it is. They have me running here and there for dumb things, but I don't really care, and I know you won't, because they can't do it to me much longer.

I'm on break today. Can you believe it? My last one. It stopped raining last night. The first time I have gone outside and not gotten wet in two weeks. The sun is even out this morning. Amazing.

Hey, I go three letters yesterday and one today from you. I hadn't heard from you in five days and then presto! I really enjoy your letters. I am waiting impatiently for the first one from you that tells me you've heard about the drop. I can't wait to see how happy it'll make you. I hope it'll make you very happy. I'm so happy right now.

Honey, I want you to stop writing on the 17th. Don't write me anymore after the 17th. I'll be leaving Phu Bai on the 23rd for Da Nang. I'll spend four days down there. I don't know why four days, but I do know I'll have to take the Pee Test and that takes a couple of days to come back then I'll leave for Ft. Lewis, Washington.

It's good that we decided not to meet in California because I have to ETS out of Ft. Lewis. I should be out by the 27th. So, if your last letter is mailed on the 17th it should get here by the 22nd or 23rd. Otherwise, I'll miss it and I don't want to miss any of your letters.

You got everything about ready? I hope so. You're probably going to be as busy as I am or more so, but it's a good kind of busy, isn't it? It also makes the time go by so fast. That's what counts, isn't it? You bet it is.

You know what, I woke up to this morning? "You make me so Very Happy". I just had to smile, because you do make me so very happy. God, I love you, Nancy!

I'm going to close for now. Keep smiling, it isn't long now. God bless you my love and I ask him to please watch over you.

All My Love,
Frank
P.S. Being short makes it. I love you, "Shorty."

This is such an awesome series of letters from Frank. He is back to being, my Frank full of life and so very happy.

12

last days are scary

Frank was experiencing lots of things in his final days in Vietnam. He was experiencing recurring dreams of us together again nearly every night. My every thought was about Frank. He was constantly on my mind and I could not wait to see him, hold him, and tell him how much I loved him. My dreams were all about him.

Of course, the Army was wanting him to re-up, but they did not have a chance of talking him into re-enlisting because four years in the Army had been quite enough for Frank and me. We wanted no more separations from each other.

Frank sent me brochures that were normally given to wives trying to get them to talk their husbands into re-enlisting. He had circled things on the brochures that he knew would make me laugh.

Fear of surviving the last few days in Vietnam had Frank taking every precaution to not let anything happen to him. I felt that fear too. We had been through so much in the last year being separated and we would not breathe easy until we were in each other's arms again. I prayed every night that the last few days would pass quickly and bring Frank home.

November 8, 1971

Dear Nancy,

Hi there. How are you today? I hope you are getting along fine and are looking forward to my coming home. I got three letters from you today.

Honey, I'm worried about getting a job and I hope we have enough money to cover us if I can't find one for a while. I just worry about things like that. It's my job as your husband to do this. It's part of the function of being a husband. Just as it's your job to take care of me and our house, it's my job to take care of the finances. You understand? Ok.

LAST DAYS ARE SCARY

You asked if I was sure that there is no mistake about the drop. I'm sure and as you know I have the orders. It's too late for them now. Decent, huh?

God, I'm crazy tonight, huh? Maybe I'm just trying so hard to be everything to you. I want everything to be right. I want to give you a good life and a good living. I want you to have everything. I want you to be proud of me and respect me. I don't ever want to fail you in any way. So, try and understand me, please. Ok? Ok!

These last few days are just dragging, aren't they? Ten months went by like fast, but thirty days seems like an eternity. So close yet...! Well, in 19 days I'll be grabbing you at the airport and I'll be so very happy. After 276 days already, we only have 19 left. I'll be there before you know it. By the time you get this, we'll only have 14 days left then when I get a reply we'll only have about 8 days left. Descent, huh!

Honey, I ask for you to bear with me for 19 more days. I'm a little worn down and worried. I promise you, I'll be my old happy self when I step off that plane. I'm confused because I don't know what to expect the next 19 days and I'm excited and don't want anything to go wrong. I'm not taking any chances.

I sleep with my war gear next to me and with my pants on at night. Things like this are making me a nervous wreck. I've spent too long from you already and now I'm not taking any chances. I just need to get out of here and get back to you and your love.

So, if I seem eccentric my last few days, I ask you to please stick by me and don't get down on me until you've seen me again and judge for yourself. I'm still me but I'm under different circumstances that you've ever seen before and when I get back to you, I'll be the same way that you're used to seeing me as.

 I have to close, Darling. Just keep faith in me and my never dying love for you. I love you so much! God bless you and please keep you safe for me. I love you, Nancy, so very much.

 All my Love is Yours,
Frank

 That was a hard letter to read. I was just as worried as Frank was about those last days he was in Vietnam. Frank wanted out of there so badly and I wanted him out of there badly. We were both saying prayers to God that the time would pass quickly, and we would be in each other's arms again.

 We both knew they were pulling more and more soldiers out of Vietnam which meant those that were still there were in more danger.

 In Frank's next letter he has calmed down some. The next letter was written one day after the one above and it really shows how up and down Frank's emotions could be from day to day. Stress and loneliness can reap havoc on our emotions. Frank and I were both feeling these same emotions. Every day our emotions seemed different.

 November 9, 1971
Dear Nancy,
 Hello, my Darling. Like the red ink? Well, it's to signify that I have nothing else but a red pen. HA! I love you, you shorty you.
 As you can probably tell, I'm in a perfectly foolish mood tonight. I've been that way since I woke this morning. I didn't sleep very well last night, and I kept having a dream. I'd wake up smile then go right back to sleep

and take up where I left off. It was one long continuous dream.

I'm starting to get the same dream or one similar to it every night. There are always only two people in it. Guess who these two are? You're right. It's only you and I, of course. Now, I know what you're thinking. No, I'm not always making love to you. Sometimes you're making love to me. HA! HA!

No seriously, I dream about us walking and talking things over between us. It'll be so good to be able to sit down with you and talk over everything together. Like we used to. Just being together again will mean so much to both of us, I think.

You're everything to me, Nancy, and I won't be me again till you're by my side once again. You see, when I left, I left the best part of me behind. I'll not be the same until I once again have my other part. That other part is you, my love. I know I may say foolish things at times and get out of sorts, but I can't truly help it over here. Still, you have stuck by me and continued to give me the one thing I need the most, Love.

Another thing you have always shown and just showing this makes me feel the strength you have given me. That is understanding. Without understanding and accepting me when I'm out of sorts, you would have given up on me long ago. You can understand when I act like an ass and try and protect me from myself by reassuring me of your love and devotion.

None of these things I have said or done is a reflection on you. It's my fault and I know this. You have not failed me in any way at all. It's me, being away from you and being so lonely so long and numerous other things combined. I could go on making excuses for my behavior, but

I know my mistakes and all I can hope for is that with you and I working together, we can overcome my faults and shortcomings. OK? OK!

I'm getting really excited Honey. In 18 days, I'll be gathering you up in my freckled arms and telling you, I love you. I'll leave Phu Bai in 14 days. Jesus, Honey, we're almost there. It seems like a miracle come true. I'm so happy. I hope you are as happy as I am. I love you so much, Nancy.

I'm gonna hafta close and try to get some sleep. I pray for you and I ask Him to keep you safe and protected for me Darling because I love you so much. Take care of yourself because you are mine and you're all I live for. I love you, Nancy, so very much.

All My Love,
Frank
P.S. "short"

Somethings are so special that they make you smile ear to ear and make you feel like the most loved person in the world as you read them, even if the words were written to you forty-seven years ago. The letter above definitely fits in that special category.

I never considered that Frank made any mistakes. In my eyes he was perfect. He was in a war zone surrounded by things that were unfathomable to me. I loved him with all of my heart and I would not let him be down. I did everything in my power to let him know that he was not alone, that I loved him, that I was being faithful to him, and that I was waiting for him. Frank was my heart and soul.

Frank is still in a great mood in his next letter.

November 10, 1971
Dear Short Wife,

LAST DAYS ARE SCARY

Nice word isn't it. I guess by now you're sick of me feeling so good, huh? I guess all I talk about anymore is getting short. Well, I tell you what. Getting short has only one purpose and that's to get myself home to you. If you get tired of hearing about that then tough! I'm gonna tell you anyway. So there. I love you, Nancy.

I imagine you are also getting tired of having to go to the post office and pick up these dumb letters from your idiot husband. Well, once again, tough! I'm getting closer to you day by day and you're going to hear how it feels. So there!

Well, there are about five of my neighbors sitting around in here and we're listening to the old radio and drinking beer and B.S.ing. They keep telling me I'm going to re-up. Well, I just smile and say nothing.

It feels good to have good friends who share your feelings and are happy for you. I can't even go into the bar and buy a drink. Everyone buys me a drink. Oh well.

Well, this is a weird letter, I guess but I'm out of things to say, so I'll say what's utmost in my mind. I love you. Please take care of yourself and pray for me, Darling. I'll be home to you soon. I promise. Then everything will be ok once and for all. God bless you and I'll see you soon my love.

All My Love,
Frank
P.S. Check out these Zip envelopes. See how they spell Cambodia and Thailand. Stupid Zips
I LOVE YOU

I think that Mr. Henderson might just have been a tad bit inebriated in the letter above, but he was happy and being funny so when I read it I smiled. Frank always made good friends with everyone he met, and people loved my "dimple-faced" husband. Everyone trusted him and knew that he would never let them down, ever.

Frank was right about the envelopes and the misspelled countries. Thailand is spelled *Thailande* and Cambodia is spelled *Cambodge*. I have several of the envelopes with the misspellings.

When I received the above letter Frank and I would only have twelve days left until he came home. It all seemed like such a dream.

13

getting closer to you

The final days apart were passing for Frank and me, but each day seemed to go too slowly. We were so ready and anxious to be together again then start our new adventure in life. Frank and I didn't care what we had to do to survive our future, we just wanted to do it holding each other's hand and looking into each other's eyes.

Frank had asked me not to write to him after November 17th because he would have already left Phu Bai for Da Nang and he would not receive letters from me.

It was so hard to break the habit of writing to him every day, but it helped that I was still receiving mail from him. I received the next letter from Frank written on November 14th about the 20th of November of 1971.

> *November 14, 1971*
> *Dear Nancy,*
> *Hello, my love. How is your day? I hope it's a beautiful day and you're happy and feeling well. Because when you get this letter you'll only have about one more week to yourself. After that hang it up. That husband of yours will be back and you won't have a moment to yourself.*
>
> *You'll have to go back to the old slave labor routine again. Washing his dirty socks, feeding him, picking up after him, and complying to his every wish. The old tedious task of being a wife. It's tedious alright but also has its advantages.*
>
> *You will be loved as no woman has ever been loved before. You will be treated like a queen. Though probably not in material things, such as lots of money, beautiful clothes, or expensive jewelry. You will be treated like a queen because of my love for you. You'll never want for love, devotion, and respect.*

GETTING CLOSER TO YOU

You'll not find a better father for the children you bear me. I'll work fourteen hours a day to give them the things a child should have. But I'll always find plenty of time to give them all the love and affection they need and deserve.

You asked if I would be okay with us having a child right away. Nancy, I would be so proud to father a child. It would make me so proud to give a child. It's something I have wanted to give you for almost four years now. For you to want me to share the parenthood of a child with you fills my heart with so much pride and love. I love you so much, Nancy.

Our time apart is closely drawing to an end. It seems like an eternity since we were together. Our own private hell is ending, at last. Needless to say, it's about time. I think if I had to go another month without you, I wouldn't make it. I guess I could, but I don't see how.

My love for you, Nancy is so real and wonderful. I can't wait till you can see just how much I do love you. I'll never let you forget how much I love you.

Honey, I'd better close. Please take care of yourself for me. God bless you and take care of you for me. I love you.

All My Love Forever,
Frank
P.S. I love you and miss you so much, "shorty"
I am enclosing a brochure given to me for you to read to encourage me to re-up. I thought you would get a kick out of this. I love you even though you hate the Army. HA!
Love, Frank

I laughed when I saw the re-up brochure that Frank sent me. He had circled promises that we knew were not true and he made funny comments by them. There was absolutely no way Frank was going to re-up and I knew it.

Although we had lived in some beautiful places, Frank and I were done with the Army. Being separated was not for us. We just wanted to be side by side for whatever the future held for us.

The next letter Frank brought home with him. It is the last letter that I wrote to him while he was in Vietnam and one of the two that he saved. The other letter from me was the one I typed to him about the kisses he owed the Credit Bureau which is in another chapter in Book Two.

Seeing my writing in this letter, I can tell how excited I was that Frank was coming home. Also, I can read in my words the fear and concern for Frank's safety in his final days.

November 17, 1971
Dearest Darling,
I Love You! Honey, I wish so much that this was the 27th instead of the 17th. I miss you so much.

Honey, you told me not to write after today, so I won't, but remember my Love is with you till my love and I both can be with you. Please, take care of yourself and hurry home to me. I Love You With All of My Heart.

Gosh, I wish these last ten days would hurry up and pass by. The thought of holding you tightly and lying beside you makes me feel so warm and content. I Love You With All of My Heart Frank and I Miss You So Much.

I made a cake for your Mom's birthday tonight and I'm going to get her a punch bowl set.

Oh, Frank, I Love You So Very, Very Much, please take care of yourself and God keep you safe. I Live For

You and I Can't Live Without You. I Love You too much to go through life without you by my side. I Love You, Frank!

Honey call me as soon as you get to the states. If our phone messes up, call my folk's house and they'll come to get me. Okay? Okay! I Love You.

Honey, I'll close for now. I Love You and I pray that God will please, please take care of you and keep you safe till I can help Him. I Love You With All of My Heart. God Bless You, Darling.

All of My Love Is Yours Forever Frank.
I Love You,
Nancy
P.S. 10 DLITA
SHORTER THAN SHORT!!
10>9>8>7>6>5>4>3>2>1>Together Again Forever!!

I was not the only one who was feeling the overwhelming excitement in those final ten days. Frank's last letter to me was written one day after I wrote the above letter and he was having a very hard time thinking and writing.

It had been a long year for us with so many emotions. I honestly can't tell you what I did those last few days. I am sure I was anxious, worried and in a daze. Frank was worried too. He was so afraid that something would happen to me even though I was in a safe place.

Thanksgiving was on November 25th of 1971, so that was a little of a distraction for me and Frank was busy processing out of Phu Bai then traveling to Da Nang for more processing, so he had distractions too.

The following letter is the last letter I received from Frank while he was in Vietnam.

November 18, 1971
Dearest Nancy,
Golly, I can't even spell Dearest any more. I guess I'm just too excited over coming home.

Today was my last working day in the Army. It didn't really seem possible. I've gotten until the 22nd to clear post and then on the 23rd, I'll leave here for Da Nang.

Good grief, we're really short. It's finally going to happen. I'm so happy! By the time you get this letter, I'll be in Da Nang.

I hope you have a very nice Thanksgiving. Eat plenty for me too. Save me some black olives. OK? OK!

Nancy, I love you so much. I can't think of anything to say except, I love you so.

Forgive me for quitting but all I can think of is in just a short time I'll be looking at you. So, goodnight my Darling and please take care and I'll see you soon. God bless you and watch over you, my love.

All My Love for You,
Frank

P.S. How about a kiss? I expect a really good one when I first see you. So be prepared.

The letter above arrived on the 24th of November after I read it, I would not hear from Frank until the phone would ring.

In the evening of November 28th, 1971, our phone rang, and I quickly answered it. I heard Frank say with his voice breaking into tears, "Nancy, I love you so much! I made it Nancy. I am nearly home."

Frank's voice was so full of emotion that I started crying and he told me, "Nancy, please don't cry. I promise you I will never leave you again."

All I could say was, "I love you, Frank. I love you, Frank." Over and over.

We finally got our emotions in check then Frank told me when he would arrive in Houston from Washington. We talked until his flight number was called then counted to three together before we hung up the phone.

After hanging up the phone, I called both our families to let them know that Frank was stateside, and I would be picking him up in Houston.

God had answered our prayers and we were so thankful.

14

a message in a letter

Frank's next letter has a beautiful message and it is very special to me. In late January of 2015, I said a prayer asking God for a new purpose for me. I was getting older and needed to have something to do for Him. At that time had been a widow for eighteen years and retired for six years. That night Frank came to me in a dream and told me, "Nancy, look in the cedar chest."

For some reason, I immediately woke up. Lying there in the darkness, I tried to figure out what Frank's words had meant. I have a cedar chest in my house but know everything that is inside it. Most of the contents are things that came from the funeral home in satchels after Frank's funeral and other special things of his.

Finally, I decided to just go back to sleep and think about it in the morning but just as I was dozing off, I remembered that there was another old cedar chest in a shed in my backyard. Quickly, I sat up in bed. No matter how hard I tried, there was no remembrance of what was in the old cedar chest.

Of course, it was still dark outside and there was not a light in the shed, so I decided to get up, get dressed, make coffee, and wait for first light. I took a cup of coffee and sat outside in the darkness on my patio anxiously waiting.

At first light, I was at the shed door. After going inside, I realized there were lots of boxes stored on top of the old cedar chest, so I moved them then opened the lid to the cedar chest. The first thing I saw in the cedar chest was a box. The box was a square about twelve inches wide by twelve inches long and eight inches deep. Frank and I had received dinner plates in the box at a wedding shower before we married.

When I removed the lid to the box, I saw letters, lots of letters. Since there was not much light in the shed, I put the lid back on the box then carried the box and headed to my game room. After sitting the box down on the table in the room, I removed the lid. The letters were tightly packed in file form on one side of the box. On the other side leaning against the letters were other letters.

I pulled out the first letter in the row of filed letters then I knew what they were. They were letters that I had received from Frank when he was in Vietnam in 1971. Reading each letter was like reading it for the first time because I did not remember one word written in them. Separation from Frank and the devastating emotions of fear for his safety that year had erased those written words from my mind after each was stored in the box.

With the eyes of a sixty-six-year-old widow rather than a twenty-one-year-old scared and fearful wife, I saw the beauty of the things my young husband had written in his letters to me and I could see each emotion he was having in his handwriting.

After reading each letter then placing it in order in the box, I realized that the last time this old cedar chest had been opened was after placing the last letter in the box that Frank had written to me from Vietnam, just shortly before he came home safely to me.

Once reading the last letter in the box then pulling back the others that were tightly filed in the box, I found a letter lying underneath the others. Thinking that it was a little strange that I had not noticed it under the others before, I sat down at the table, opened the envelope, took out the letter then began to read it. I was totally amazed at the beauty of what Frank had said in the letter.

When I finished reading it, I realized that there was a message to me from Frank not just in 1971 but also that day in late January of 2015. Also, I realized that God had intended for this letter to be the last one for me to find and read even though it was not the last one that Frank wrote to me. This letter has an eternal message of a love that is never-ending even after death.

Also, I realized that God had a purpose for me to share these letters. I do not know that purpose and I just pray that am fulfilling His purpose.

The first part of the letter is typed, so I will not italicize it, but the second part is handwritten, and it will be italicized. Also, Frank wrote a poem for me and included it in this letter.

> November 4, 1971
> Dear Nancy,
> Hi there, Beautiful. How is every little thing with you today? As you can probably guess, I am on C.Q. tonight. It is my turn again. It is now 11:15 pm at night and I am sitting here listening to the mortars go off (ours of course). It has been a pretty dull night so far. One guy came in with a spider bite on his arm and the 85th EVAC Hospital wouldn't take him because of so many emergency cases tonight. I guess someone is really getting their stuff blown away.
>
> Bob (from Okie) brought me in two beers and I just went and got another one, so my poor mouth wouldn't go too dry before morning. So, now I am sitting down to write you a long letter. How about that????
>
> *You seem to have a premonition about me getting out early. You got E.S.P powers you did not tell me about? Well, if you do then why don't you get me home now???? HA! HA!*
>
> *I really look forward to your first letter after you find out about our drop. Either tomorrow or the next day, I should be getting one about it. I wish I could have been there to see your face when you heard about it. I bet you were happy. I certainly was. All I could think about was*

how happy you would be. I am so happy, Nancy. We will be together in only 23 days. This time it won't be for 30 days or 45 days, it will be forever.

Just think, to never have to part again. Never stand in an airport and say goodbye again. I will never have to see your tears again as I leave. I will never have to sit on that damn plane and look out trying to catch that last glimpse of you before I leave. I will never have to try and tell you how much I love you in a letter. All the things that have been bothering us for so long will never bother us again. That has to be wonderful. I love you so much, Nancy.

I am getting so excited that I can't sleep at night. I lay in my bed and toss and turn all night. I try to think of something else, but I can't. The whole world is based on you and our home. I feel so good that I don't ever want to stop thinking of it and I know that thinking of it is only minute compared to the feeling I will have when I once again hold you in my arms. A warm glow just surrounds me when I think about it. I love you so much.

By the way, I have been having some nasty thoughts about you lately. It may sound nasty to the other people, but it feels so nice to me. I can't control myself much longer. My dreams are taking me over. You and I fit together so nicely in my dreams. (I really am horrible aren't I?) HA! HA! It will be so nice when dreams give away to reality. I guess you think I am some kind of sex nut, don't you? Well, to tell you the truth, I am, but I guess you knew that already didn't you?

I am only kidding, and you know it. I dream about you and I walking together on the side of a hill and during our walk, we sit down and talk. On this hill, we can see for miles and miles and there is no other soul there but you and me. We talk about our future and our plans.

I am really concerned about what I am going to do when I get out. But I keep thinking about having you near and us talking out plans out, that I feel confident that we can work it all out. I need you to help with me in figuring out what I am going to do and such. I want your help because you know me, and you know what I think, feel, and want.

That is why I am looking so forward to our being alone because if we are alone we can do some serious thinking and talking and work out these things before our parents can ask what we are going to do. I wrote my folks and said I wanted only you at the airport to meet me and I think they will understand. So, what are we waiting for?????

I am sending you a copy of my orders, so you can see them. After all, it isn't every day your husband gets the orders to the key to happiness, is it? I just thought you would like to see them. OK? OK!

Honey, I'm going to finish this letter up in pen, because I just can't get any feeling from that mill. I have so many things to say to you when I get to you again. It's been a long lonely struggle and it's almost over now. I want to hold you and assure you that I love you and I'll never leave you again. This I promise you and you know I mean it.

We are two people that were made to live with one another. We were made to share our lifetimes as one. It's an evenly balanced scale. We both needed each other in order to live a full happy life. I could never be happy again if I didn't know you were mine and that you always wanted me to be all yours. We have the gift of life.

Love. With love anything is possible. I have you and just having you means that my life has a happiness that can't be compared to anything.

Being over here has been hell for the both of us. Yet, I can't really gripe because all the time you remained faithful to me and your love for me hasn't flickered a bit. It's grown stronger, just as my love for you has bloomed into a love that is unbeatable. Now we have a full happy life ahead and we are both mature and we both realize just how wonderful our love has become.

Our love was like a new wine. It's still wine, but it's weak. Once it's been aged and tested it's not only wine but great wine. The same holds true with our love. It's aged and been tested over and over and now it's perfection. Can you understand what I'm trying to say? I'm trying to tell you that Honey, we are one and nothing will ever part us again. Not death or anything else.

Our love is a forever thing and it's the most beautiful forever thing God has ever created. I'm trying to convey my love to you through this paper and pen and I only hope you can understand how I feel and realize what I'm trying to say to you. I love you, Nancy.

God bless you, my love, and keep you safe for me. I'll be home soon, and everything will be ok. Take care Honey and think of me and don't worry about anything.

All My Love for Eternity,
Frank
P.S. I'm counting.
Nancy,
In my bunk at night, I lay,
just counting the hours in a day.
For soon it will be all over,
then nothing but blue skies and green clover.

*All the long lonely nights of the past
will end when we are together at last.
I think of you and how your beautiful eyes shine,
when I look at you and lay it all on the line.
My love is for only you and it's nice.
I wouldn't change that love for any price.
Our love is so wonderful and fulfilling,
and will always be, God willing.
He has given us something that is beyond compare.
He has given us something that only we share.
For you, I'll gladly die in this lonely land,
because my life is you and you've given me your hand,
and said, "Frank, by you I'll always stand."
You said, "I'll love you for an eternity",
and you have as anyone can see.
I am what I am because you are what you are,
and together, as one, we can go so far.
You've given me yourself, your love, your life,
and I thank God that you, Nancy, are my wife.
I love you, Nancy.
Frank*

 A message to me in a letter in 1971 letting me know that we had become one heart and soul for eternity that even death could not part.

 In 2015 this same message would be a gift from God in the answer to a prayer for purpose followed by a dream in which Frank asked me to look in a cedar chest that I remembered hidden away in a shed in my backyard.

 Forty-four years these letters had set undisturbed waiting for me to ask God for a purpose in prayer. Thinking He knew I would and thinking He had a plan.

A MESSAGE IN A LETTER

I have now shared all of the letters that Frank wrote to me while he was in Vietnam in 1971. Originally when I read these letters, I decided to end this Memoir with these letters but after typing each letter and rereading them, I realized how worried Frank was about what he would do after he came home.

Frank was an extraordinary man and he would do extraordinary things, so our love story will continue...

15

leaving the army behind us

Frank processed out of Fort Lewis in Washington state then called me on the telephone. After we talked, he got on an airplane, which flew him to Houston Intercontinental Airport.

After talking with Frank then hanging up the telephone, I could not quit smiling. We were actually out of the Army. I was no longer a soldier's wife and there would be no more war and separation. I was now Frank's wife for the first time without the Army hovering over us.

It is a strange feeling to go from the emotions of terrible fear and worry to those of excitement and happiness. I was so thankful and kept thanking God over and over for bringing Frank home safely to me.

Our suitcases were packed, except for a few last minute things. When Frank let me know approximately his arrival home day, I had started packing our suitcases for our Second Honeymoon.

It was so unbelievable to know that we were now free to just go wherever we wanted to go without the burden of worry in the back of our minds about us being separated and Frank having to leave again.

We would never have to stand in an Airport and feel like ours heart would break into pieces as we held each other tightly and kissed goodbye before Frank would have to turn then quickly walk away from me to leave on an airplane.

There would be no more crying myself to sleep at night while holding Frank's pillow tightly after writing him a letter telling him how much I loved him. I could now hold him tightly every night while telling him how much I loved him.

The telephone could now ring and there would be no fear when answering it. A knock at the door would not cause me to lose my breath and a pounding heart as I went to answer it. Fear and anxiety would not rule our lives anymore and we thanked God for that.

Frank and I knew without God's loving arms around us, His amazing grace, and His answer to our prayers, we would not have made it through one moment of being apart from each other. We would never forget God's love and mercy for us.

So many thoughts went through my mind as I got dressed, finished packing our suitcases, and loaded them into our Volkswagen then drove to the airport. I really do not remember the drive to the airport, but I do remember parking the car and running into the building which held the terminal where Frank's plane would unload.

There was not a lot of sitting in the chairs in the terminal lobby for me while waiting for Frank's plane to land. I spent most of that time looking out the windows in anticipation of getting the first glimpse of his plane coming out of the skies to land.

Finally, I saw his plane come into sight and land. As the plane taxied to the terminal, I thought my heart would pound out of my chest as I quickly walked to the terminal ramp where the passengers would walk into the terminal from then I saw him behind others coming down the ramp.

When Frank saw me, his face instantly broke into the biggest grin. It took all the restraint in me to stand there waiting for him to make his way through the crowd coming down the ramp. Then, Frank dropped his bag, ran to me, and I jumped into his arms then we embraced tightly and kissed while he lifted me off my feet as we twirled round and round. We just could not stop kissing each other as tears ran down our cheeks, but they were tears of total happiness.

Once we decided to quit kissing and hugging each other, Frank gently placed my feet back on the ground then we noticed a crowd standing around us with big smiles on their faces. Frank took my hand into his and we walked hand in hand to the baggage claim area to retrieve his duffel bag.

After retrieving the duffel bag, Frank and I left the building and walked to our car. Once we got in the car, we decided that we were really hungry. It was about 6:00 a.m. in the morning when we stopped at a pancake house to eat breakfast.

I do not think two people could have sat closer together than we did in the booth that our waitress had led us to. The waitress asked us if we were newlyweds then we told her all about what that day meant for us. She was so happy for us then told everyone in the room. When we got through eating and got up to go pay, the waitress told us that the manager said our meal was free. We thanked her and the manager for their kindness then we left.

When we got into the car again, Frank asked, "Where are we headed to Nancy?"

I answered, "Van Vleck."

Frank looked at me smiling then asked, "Van Vleck? Why are we going to Van Vleck?"

Looking deeply into his eyes, I answered, "We need to go see your folks because they need to see you are okay and hug you too. It has been a long year for them too, full of worry and fear. Once we have visited with them a while then we can go wherever you want, Dimples."

Frank laughed and shook his head as he replied, "Nancy, I love you so much. That was not the plan, but you are so right. Get over here closer and kiss me."

Of course, I kissed him but there was no way that we could get any closer because I was practically sitting in his lap as we drove out of Houston on our way to Van Vleck.

Soon we arrived at Frank's folk's home then stood on their porch and rang the doorbell. Frank's mom answered the door and she was so surprised. She opened the screen door then hugged Frank tightly. Frank's mom was a very strong woman who I had never seen cry, but her eyes welled up with tears as she hugged her oldest child and first-born son in her arms.

Frank's dad was at work, so we decided to stay until he got home and eat supper with them. I cannot recall where Frank's little sister was, but I think she might have been down for a nap when we arrived at Frank's folk's home.

When we got into the house, Frank asked his mom if he could take a shower. Frank told her he wanted to take a hot shower and get Vietnam off of his skin and it had been forever since he felt really clean. Of course, she told him it was okay, and she would make some coffee while he showered, so Frank headed to the back shower in their home while I went to get him some clean clothes out of his suitcase in our car.

After retrieving Frank some clothes from our car, I took them into the bathroom where Frank was taking a shower. When I opened the door to the bathroom, Frank was standing there in his birthday suit then looked at me smiling with those incredible dimples. I closed the bathroom door behind me, laid his clean clothes on the counter, and smiled back at him.

Timeout...

Frank and I walked into the kitchen together hand in hand, got two cups of coffee, and joined his mom in the den. We visited and had coffee then visited more when Frank's dad came home from work. Frank's mom and I fixed supper together then we all ate, cleaned up, and visited some more.

After Frank and I left his folk's home, we decided to go to our little white house in Van Vleck to spend the night. I remember every beautiful loving moment of that night, but it's a memory for only me.

Frank and I had all the time in the world together for the rest of our lives, and we knew that we could leave the next morning at whatever time we wanted. There was no one telling us to hurry because we only had so much time to be together.

We had left the Army behind us, forever.

16

deciding our future

Upon waking the next morning, I reached behind me for Frank, but he was not there. I felt a deep panic inside me as my eyes searched the room for Frank. *Had this all been some dream and he was not home yet?*

Jumping out of bed, I grabbed my robe, and put it on then I could smell the aroma of bacon cooking. Frank was not only home but in our kitchen cooking bacon.

I happy-danced down the hall to the kitchen, and when I entered the room, Frank said, "Good Morning, wife. How do you want your eggs?"

With a smile as big as Texas on my face, I answered, "Over easy with lots of husband's hugs and kisses."

Frank smiled at me with his big ole dimples then pulled me into his arms as he hugged and kissed me. For some reason, at that very moment, I did not even care about eating breakfast anymore, but he would not let me pull him away from the kitchen, so I decided to release let him out of the bear hug I had him in then get the eggs out of the refrigerator for him.

While Frank finished cooking the bacon then taking it out of the frying pan, I made toast in the toaster while he fried our eggs. We fixed our plates and then sat down at the kitchen table to eat. We were like two giddy lovesick kids again, talking and laughing, as we ate breakfast.

While Frank was in Vietnam, we had made get-away plans to go to my Grandfather's farm, but these plans had to be changed because it was hunting season. Since many others could be there now to hunt or might show up at any time, we decided to start driving north in the Volkswagen without a plan and see where we would end up.

After we cleaned up the kitchen together, we showered, got dressed, and loaded our bags back into the Volkswagen then off we headed to places unknown. As we headed north, taking the back roads through lots of little towns and stopping to look at interesting things along the way, we talked about everything.

At lunchtime, we stopped at a little grocery store, bought soft drinks, bread, lunch meat, cheese slices, mayo, and chips. When we came upon a small rest stop on the side of the road, we stopped. We sat at the picnic table, making sandwiches, laughing, eating, and talking. Once we finished eating, we cleaned up our mess, then headed back on the road again with our-trip-to-anywhere-as-long-as-we-were-alone-and-together.

When evening came, we stopped at a motel to spend the night. We took our bags into our room then went back outside to sit on the grass behind the motel so we could watch the sunset. I don't remember the name of the town or the motel, but I remember that the motel set on a hill. The thing I do remember was sitting in front of Frank leaning back against him with his arms wrapped around me as we sat there staring at the sky. For the first time that day we did not talk, we just sat there in silence watching the sun go down. I will never forget the peacefulness and feeling of love we shared in those quiet moments.

The next day after a trip to a store to buy donuts for breakfast, we headed out on the road again, stopping only for gasoline and another noon picnic. As we traveled down the highway, we were making plans for our future, talking about all of our options until we came up with a fantastic idea which was doable if we worked hard together. As night fell, we ended up in Lubbock, Texas, where we stopped at another motel to spend the night.

Frank and I had a friend who lived in Lubbock that we had met in Okinawa. He was one of the single GIs who would spend lots of time at our home. We looked him up in the phone book then gave him a call. He was excited to hear from us. We made plans to pick him up in the morning then drive to Palo Duro Canyon, located between Lubbock and Amarillo, Texas.

It is sometimes referred to as the Grand Canyon of Texas and is the second largest Canyon in the nation. We spent the day walking around in the canyon then we took our friend out to eat in a restaurant in Lubbock that evening before taking him home then returning to our motel room for the night.

The next morning Frank and I headed out on a different path and the new direction was south. We headed back to Van Vleck, but we would not travel south the same way we had gone north. We saw no fun in that. Texas is a vast state, so you can always find a different path to take. Frank and I had made our plans for our future on our trip north, so our trip south would be one of looking at the scenery and more picnics. We would also make a quick stop in College Station, Texas, to pick up some forms from the college.

Believe it or not, after five days on the road, we were ready to get home to our little white frame house in Van Vleck. It was early December, and we had lots of people to see and things to do before Christmas. Our last Christmas together had been one full of fear and trying to deal with the separation from each other that was ahead of us, but this Christmas would be one of thankfulness, clinging to each other, and celebration. We could not wait to put up a tree, spend time with family, and celebrate together.

When we returned home, we visited with our families, and if asked what our plans for the future were, we told them about our future plans. No one questioned our decisions. I think they knew that we were very firm in our choices and we would not change our minds.

DECIDING OUR FUTURE

We had stopped in College Station on our way to Van Vleck to pick up a form for married student housing. It would take at least a full semester for us to get approved and into married student housing. Frank would attend Wharton County Junior College for the Spring semester of 1972 on the GI Bill which would pay for his books and tuition with some money left for living expenses. We had saved quite a bit of money while Frank was in Vietnam and knew we could live off of it for a while. Knowing how to cut back and spend very little money had been part of our life together since the day we married. Early on in our marriage, we had made some costly mistakes, and these mistakes were still fresh in our memories.

Frank did not want me to work, and we argued about that in private, but he would only agree to me substituting at the schools in Van Vleck. Before Frank registered with Wharton County Junior College and arranged his schedule, he made a trip to Phillips 66 Refinery in Old Ocean, Texas to apply for a job, but they were not interested in hiring a Vietnam Veteran even though Frank had family that worked in the plant. Having served a year in the unpopular Vietnam War/Conflict made it hard for soldiers returning home to get a job because of the unfair baggage that the war attached to them.

Wharton County Junior College was a thirty-mile trip one way from Van Vleck so, Frank would need the car to drive back and forth to school most days, but he could also catch a school bus in Bay City which was provided by the college. Since we lived only a couple of blocks from the Van Vleck schools, I could walk to substitute teach. On days that I needed the car, we decided I would take Frank to Bay City, which was six miles from Van Vleck so he could catch the bus. The problem with Frank riding the bus was that it only ran once a day to Wharton in the morning and once a day to Bay City in the afternoon. Depending on his schedule, it could be that he would have to sit and wait for a class to begin or wait for the bus to arrive in the afternoon to take him back to Bay City.

Christmas time was so beautiful. We bought a live tree, decorated it with lights, ornaments, and icicles. We cooked together, making fudge and cookies, we went shopping with our folks, we went to Christmas parties at Uncle and Aunts homes, and we spent many nights lying with pillows and a blanket on the living room rug, listening to our Reel to Reel and holding each other tightly, sometimes actually sleeping there all night. Frank and I would not have gifts under the tree for each other that year because we had decided that we already had the best gift we could ever receive from God and that gift was, we were together again.

Christmas Eve, we spent with Frank's folks, then at the stroke of midnight, we drove six hours straight to get to my Grandmother's home in Hico, Texas to celebrate Christmas Day with my folks. This drive would be our first all-night drive to celebrate with both our families, but it would not be the last. We would do this exact thing every Christmas only alternating which day we would spend with our folks. We enjoyed the drive together and looked forward to it each year.

Frank and I rang in the New Year together, and it was extra special for us. January had always been the month when Frank would be telling me goodbye at the airport in Houston but not in 1972 or any other year for the rest of our lives together. The next time Frank and I would go to the airport would be to fly together to Oklahoma City on a company business trip, probably fifteen years later.

Frank enrolled at Wharton County Junior College and looked for weekend work, while I substituted at Van Vleck Schools. Soon, Frank got a part-time job working Saturdays only with a flying service located right outside of Wharton.

At night I helped Frank with his college Algebra which he had decided was some foreign language which had nothing to do with real adding, subtracting and multiplying. Math was just not Frank's subject, but History, Health, Government, English, and Spanish were right up his alley. Frank never forgot anything he read, and he read all the time, on the other hand, Nancy Lou was not gifted with that kind of memory unless she was interested in what she was learning, but numbers were her thing.

Now, we had a routine going at our home in Van Vleck, and we loved every minute of it. When the Spring Semester was over, the flying service offered Frank a full-time job for the summer, which was awesome. Frank had decided to not take Summer Semester classes at the Wharton County Junior College to save his GI Bill because he had been approved and accepted for the Fall Semester at Texas A&M. Also, our married student housing was approved, and we would be able to move into our apartment right before the Fall Semester began. We were so excited. Our plans were happening just the way we had dreamed they would.

During the Summer of 1972, we took many trips to the beach on Frank's day off, had friends over for Supper, and spent time with our families.

We had looked into adoption, but we did not have enough money, and it took a long time to adopt a child, so we decided to wait, save as much money as we could, and see what might happen naturally. We knew that God would decide when we would have a child whether or not it was through adoption or naturally. God had never failed us in any way at any time.

In late August of 1972, Frank and I loaded up a U-Haul Truck we had rented and was sitting in front of our little white frame home in Van Vleck, Texas. When we had loaded all of our belongings and furniture inside the truck, we walked hand in hand to the landlord's home next door to turn in the keys to the house.

Frank got into the truck to drive it to College Station, and I followed him driving our Volkswagen. As we drove away from that little white frame home, tears ran down my face. That home had seen many tears, worry, and heartache, but also extreme happiness and true love. It was the first house that we had lived in together in the states as a married couple, and we knew that we would never forget it.

Not long ago, I drove to Van Vleck to see that little white frame house, but it was not there. It made me sad until I found out that it is still in Van Vleck. The house had been bought and moved to the other side of town, so I made another trip to see it. As I stopped on the road in front of it, I could see in my mind every detail of the inside of the house as I mentally walked through it. I did not get out of my car and go to the door because I wanted to remember it just as it was so long ago.

As Frank and I pulled into College Station about lunchtime that hot August day, we were ready to get the key to our apartment, unpack our belongings then begin our new exciting journey as Aggies at Texas A&M. We could not imagine what amazing things we would encounter in College Station. God had big plans and surprises for us.

Stay Tuned!

Nancy Lou Henderson writes. A lot. Some of the items she writes are funny and irreverent. Other pieces are introspective and thought-provoking. And let's not even get started on the ones that will make you a blubbering mess because they are so heart-wrenching and poignant.

That's why you have to *stay tuned*!
Connect with Nancy.
Follow her blog.
Find her on Facebook.
Tweet her on Twitter.
Use these links to connect.

Ⓦ *www.nancylouhenderson.com*

◼ facebook.com/nancy.henderson.39

🐦 @nlhende49

Please help us bring awareness to Nancy's work. Tell everyone you know how much you enjoyed this book. Ask your local bookstore to stock it. And please-please-please give it a good review online and on social media. It's kind gestures like these that help Nancy and other independent authors to carry on bringing you such wonderful and heart-felt work for your enjoyment and edification. Thank you!

Also by
Nancy Lou Henderson

Love & Marriage:
The Love Story of Nancy &
Frank: Book I

War & Commitment:
The Love Story of Nancy &
Frank: Book II

A Very Special Preview of Faith & Eternity: The Love Story of Nancy & Frank: Book IV

1

big bubbles & packing beetle

After collecting the keys to our apartment, Frank and I headed to College View Apartments in search of our new home.

These apartments sat across the road from the College Campus, thus how they got their name. The buildings were two-story old Army barracks converted into eight apartment units.

On the front of the building, there were two separate entrances. Each entrance had a two-step small concrete porch that led to a screen door. When you entered through the screen door, there was a small entryway and on either side of this entryway was a door. Each of these two doors was the front door of an apartment.

Facing the screen door in the entryway was a staircase leading to the next story where there was another landing with two more doors on either side of it which were front doors to two more apartments. The entrance on the other side of the front of the apartment building was an exact repeat of this description.

Frank and I lucked out and received the keys to a downstairs apartment on the left side front of the building. Our front door was on the right of the entry hall which meant we were in an interior apartment. We would not have to haul our furniture up the stairs. There was only one obvious disadvantage to our apartment, and that was the ninety-degree turn that had to made to get furniture through the screen door then into the front door of our apartment. Not to mention how small the entryway was before the stairs started upward to the next landing.

Our couch was unique in the fact that it was a couch that made a bed, but not like the ones that have a pullout bed. Instead, it was a folding couch. To make it into a bed you would grab hold of the seat then pull it upward as the back of it slid down looking like the seat. Next, you would give a little push on the lifted seat until hearing a clicking sound then the actual seat of the couch would lay back down flat again. Thinking that description of how that couch worked is as clear as mud, but I gave it my best shot.

When we got ready to move the couch and mattresses into the apartment, it took some engineering to get them through the screen door then inside the front door, accomplished only through the help of two of my brothers. That couch decided to open up, slide around trying to make a bed while the box spring mattress drug against the top of the door frame. Lots of strong words were said that day by all trying to help us move our stuff into our apartment.

The apartment was small, but for $40.00 a month it was just the right price for us. There was a small living room/dining room with an opening at the back of the room leading

PREVIEW: TIME & DISTANCE

into the kitchen. The kitchen was more like a hall with the sink cabinet unit, above sink cabinets, and apartment stove on one side with the refrigerator on the opposite side. When the refrigerator door was open it, nearly touched the sink cabinet unit on the other side of the room (hall).

We had two bedrooms with a small door-less cubbyhole between them. The bedroom doors faced each other. Across from this cubbyhole was another small cubbyhole just big enough for our washing machine to fit in. The door which led to the bathroom was next to the back-side wall of the washer cubbyhole. The largest bedroom could hold a queen-sized bed, but one side had to be pushed against the wall, leaving space in the room for a small dresser.

We did not have air conditioning, a dishwasher or dryer, but we did have our own washing machine. There were several huge clotheslines in the backyard of the building, but since there were no back doors on the building, I would be washing our clothes, putting them into a basket, going out the front door, and walking around to the back of the building to hang them on the clothesline to dry. There would not be anymore more sailing the clothes down the stairs, just a little basket-hauling-exercising-walking around to the back of the building.

The inside of the walls of the apartment had been painted white. Even the metal three-sided shower in the bathroom was painted white and looked brand new. The shower did not have a door on it, but with a spring-loaded shower rod, a shower curtain could be hung on the opening to the shower. We did not have a bathtub, so I was glad we had a washing machine, even though I would miss "Boogie Shoe" washing our laundry. Of course, I would take the radio with me to hang out the clothes on the clothesline and dance the whole time.

All of the floors in the apartment were tile, and I was pleasantly surprised to see that they were all tiled with the same color and type of tile that was in our homes in Okinawa. I could not wait to strip those floors with lye water then make them shine.

Finally, after many hours of moving in our belongs into the new apartment then unpacking, we were ready to go get something to eat. Frank and I drove to a burger place and got hamburgers, fries, and some drinks then drove home to eat them in our new home. After we finished eating, the next thing on our list was to shower then go to bed. The next story is about how that worked out.

"Bubbles"

Frank had come up with a well thought out plan since the day we married which he called "Christening the House". He thought that every new home needed christening, as soon as possible. Of course, Frank never ever forgot about this no matter how long, and hard the move in was. Although not disagreeing with him at all, I thought after a long day of driving, moving in, lifting heavy things, and unpacking that it might be okay to wait a day or two. Anyway, back to the story.

My sweet husband looked at me after we had finished eating then told me that I looked very tired and he thought that I should take the first shower in our new home. Being exactly that tired, I did not even argue with him about it but went straight to the bedroom, got a change of clothes, and headed to the shower. On the way, Mr. Dimples did ask me if I needed any help in the shower, but I assured him with a smile that I could handle it all by myself and all would be fine.

Earlier in the afternoon, I hung up the shower curtain, and a shower caddy on the shower head then put the soap and shampoo in it. While doing that, I noticed how awesome the white paint looked on the inside of the shower. It was clean and had a slickness to it.

PREVIEW: TIME & DISTANCE

Since we did not have an exhaust fan in the bathroom, I slightly opened the small window in the bathroom to let out some of the steam from the shower then I turned on the water in the shower, undressed, and entered the shower. The hot water felt really awesome as I put my head under the water to wet my hair then applied some shampoo to it. I stood there with my eyes closed while scrubbing my hair then rinsing it under the warm water before repeating the whole process one more time and then opening my eyes.

Once opening my eyes and looking straight ahead through the steam cloud hovering in the shower, I was dumbfounded by what I saw there. Bubbles! Large bubbles were coming out of the shower wall towards me! Quickly, I opened the shower curtain then screamed for Frank to come into the bathroom.

After some rustling sounds, he came running into the bathroom, pulled back the shower curtain wearing only a big smile on his dimpled-face asking, "Nancy, did you decide you need me to wash your back?"

Laughing while pointing to the walls, I told him, "Really Dimples? We have bubbles! Big bubbles!"

These bubbles were amazing! If you pushed on one of them, it would go down, and another one would pop up close by! The paint on the shower was, evidently the same as what the walls in the apartment had been painted with and, the shower had not been cleaned or primed for paint before being painted.

Of course, Frank's next words were, "Nancy Lou, you wanna pop 'em together?"

As I looked at his beautiful smile with those dimples, I knew that was exactly what we were going to do. No bubble would be left unpopped! Let's just say, lots of laughing and lots of bubbles popped.

The shower was actually a big mess, and we would have to peel many layers of paint off the shower walls before sand-ing then cleaning them with bleach before we could paint the shower with real metal paint.

Frank and I had settled into our new apartment when he registered for school. He and I were both looking for jobs. Of course, I was back to practicing my typing trying to get a job on the school campus. The jobs required that I should be able to type at least fifty words per minute, and we all know from the past how great my typing was. Of course, Frank would not even consider the possibility of me working in any jobs having to do with waitressing, grocery stores, convenience stores, etc.

After a short time, Frank got a job at a Totem convenience store near our apartment. They would work his schedule around his college courses, but I was still trying to pass the typing test. Two of my brothers were also attending school at Texas A&M and lived in the College View Apartments with their wives.

Grady's wife, Tish, worked on the campus and when Jimmy's wife, Connie, got a job on campus they needed someone to babysit my niece, I decided to do that for the Fall semester. Frank and I adored our niece. She was nearly a year old and just precious.

It was the Fall Semester at Texas A&M University, and football was in full swing. Frank and I attended yell practices, the bonfire, and all of the home football games. Frank had a student pass which was part of his tuition which would get him into the football games, and he could also buy one cheap date ticket for me.

If the Aggies played away from College Station, we would get together with my brothers and sisters-in-law at one of our apartments, eat snacks and listen to the game on the radio. Listening to the Aggie game on the radio was always so much fun which included a bunch of hollering and Whooping when the Aggies played well or scored a touchdown. Oh, I don't want to forget the Greatest part of an Aggie football game, when the Aggies score you kiss your date, hubby, or wife.

The yell practices were always held at midnight, thus the name "Midnight Yell Practice". We did some fun things getting to these practices.

"Packing Beetle"

Well, as you already know Frank and I were the owners of a 1970 Super Beetle. This Volkswagen was designed to carry five people sort of comfortably. Truthfully, it would really depend on the size of the people.

The Super Beetle had bucket seats in the front and a bench seat in the back. Behind this bench seat was a small compartment which ran the length of the width of the bench for storage. Whew, that was quite a sentence full. Anyway, back to the story.

It was raining this particular Friday night. Normally we would all walk together to the Midnight Yell Practice since our apartment buildings were just across the street from the campus. Not wanting to get wet on the walk to the yell practice, we decided to all pile into the Super Beetle to drive to the stadium. There were ten of us but through a little ingenuity and cramming, we managed to get everyone inside the car.

One small person crammed into the space behind the bench backseat, three people sat on the bench seat with three people in their laps, the passenger front bucket seat had one person sitting with another in their lap, and Mr. Dimples sat alone in the driver's seat to drive the Super Beetle.

You might wonder why we did not take two cars are a bigger car, well that was because of the small amount of parking on the campus at the time. The Super Beetle was little, so we could get into small unusual places to park.

After we were all crammed in the car, Frank shut the passenger door then ran around the front of the car to get in to drive. He laughed the whole way. Now we were like sardines in a can with everyone Whooping and laughing. When Frank started the Super Beetle, I really was not sure, as he put it into drive if it would actually be able to pull forward with all of the weight inside it, but it did.

It was so noisy inside the car that I am sure you could hear us coming for blocks. Frank told us, "You all duck down if you see a policeman, I can't afford to get a ticket."

Well now, this caused more laughter, and then everyone started trying to duck down every time we saw a car. We all even leaned into the turns like we were riding on a roller coaster.

Finally, we made it to the stadium, and Frank found a parking spot. I think it quite possibly was on a sidewalk, but I'll never tell. Frank got out of the car, laid down his seat, then came around to the passenger door, opened the door, so those two more people could get out then laid that seat down. Next, the three people in laps of those sitting on the bench backseat got out of the vehicle which allowed the bench seat sitters to exit.

Only one more person was still in the Super Beetle, and he was in the space behind the bench backseat. Frank was laughing as he pulled the lever on that backseat and the guy crammed in there rolled out. Pretty sure that guy was my brother, Grady.

When we all got to the stadium and took our place in the crowd of Aggies there, we were probably the loudest Aggies there that night, but who could actually tell, all Aggies are loud at Midnight Yell Practice.

Hullabaloo caneck! caneck! Farmers Fight! We are the Aggies the Aggies are We! Whoop!

About the Author

NANCY LOU HENDERSON was born and raised in Texas, where she met and married her soulmate, Frank, when they were both eighteen years old. Since Frank was in the Army when they married, they lived in Massachusetts then Okinawa before Frank went to Vietnam in 1971. After twenty-nine years of marriage at the age of forty-seven, Nancy became a forever widow in 1997 and has continued to be devoted to her soulmate. At age sixty-five and after a prayer to God for a renewal of purpose, her prayer was answered in a dream that sent her to a cedar chest containing a box of letters that would be her inspiration to write a memoir of her life.

Made in the USA
Lexington, KY
11 November 2019